Saint Dominic's Way of Life

D1274987

Saint Dominic's Way of Life

A Path to Knowing and Loving God

Patrick Mary Briscoe, OP
and
Jacob Bertrand Janczyk, OP

Our Sunday Visitor
Huntington, Indiana

Nihil Obstat
Rev. Andrew Hofer, OP
Censor Librorum

Imprimatur
✠ Kevin C. Rhoades
Bishop of Fort Wayne-South Bend
April 14, 2021

Imprimi potest
Very Rev. Kenneth R. Letoile, OP,
Prior Provincial Dominican Friars Province of Saint Joseph
March 4, 2021

Except where noted, the Scripture citations used in this work are taken from the *Revised Standard Version of the Bible — Second Catholic Edition* (Ignatius Edition), copyright © 1965, 1966, 2006 National Council of the Churches of Christ in the United States of America. Used by permission. All rights reserved.

Every reasonable effort has been made to determine copyright holders of excerpted materials and to secure permissions as needed. If any copyrighted materials have been inadvertently used in this work without proper credit being given in one form or another, please notify Our Sunday Visitor in writing so that future printings of this work may be corrected accordingly.

Copyright © 2021 by Patrick Mary Briscoe, OP and Jacob Bertrand Janczyk, OP

26 25 24 23 22 21   1 2 3 4 5 6 7 8 9

All rights reserved. With the exception of short excerpts for critical reviews, no part of this work may be reproduced or transmitted in any form or by any means whatsoever without permission from the publisher. For more information, visit: www.osv.com/permissions.

Our Sunday Visitor Publishing Division
Our Sunday Visitor, Inc.
200 Noll Plaza
Huntington, IN 46750
www.osv.com
1-800-348-2440

ISBN: 978-1-68192-939-2 (Inventory No. T2677)
1. RELIGION—Christianity—Saints & Sainthood
2. RELIGION—Christian Living—Spiritual Growth
3. RELIGION—Christianity—Catholic

eISBN: 978-1-68192-940-8
LCCN: 2021936805

Cover design: Lindsey Riesen
Cover art: The Crosiers
Interior design: Amanda Falk
Interior art: Saint Dominic in Prayer, El Greco – Museum of Fine Arts Boston. Public Domain image, Wikipedia

PRINTED IN THE UNITED STATES OF AMERICA

To our Mother in heaven, the Queen of Preachers, and to our mothers on earth

Do not lay up for yourselves treasures on earth, where moth and rust consume and where thieves break in and steal, but lay up for yourselves treasures in heaven, where neither moth nor rust consumes and where thieves do not break in and steal. For where your treasure is, there will your heart be also.

Matthew 6:19–21

Contents

Preface

Saint Dominic lived in a world that had lost touch with the real. He didn't discover this until, as a young priest, he embarked on a mission (that failed) to arrange a royal marriage. Traveling from his native Spain to Scandinavia, a canon distant from his cathedral, Dominic experienced firsthand the plight of many who had succumbed to widespread falsehoods and seductive ideologies and devastating lies.

This tore at his priestly heart.

UNDONE BY DUALISM

As Dominic passed through the South of France, the stronghold of the Albigensian heresy (described in chapter 2 of this beautiful book), he came in contact with people who had renounced Christianity in favor of a cult claiming to make better sense. Yet, appallingly, in order to adhere to the tenets of this new religion, followers were forced to forfeit their own humanity, for Albigensianism considered material creation to be the human being's main enemy. The meaning of life, for Albigensians, consisted in liberating the soul from the captivity of the body. Accordingly, anything that served the purposes of the "flesh" — such as marriage and procreation and family and eating — was to be rejected. Sanctity insisted on release from matter. This meant that suicide stood as a virtue in Albigensianism, and the most commendable form of suicide was self-induced starvation.

All this may seem quite quaint — primitive and passé. But fast-forward to the inconceivable events of 2020. This preface is being written while the world writhes in the throes of the ongoing coronavirus pandemic. In August 2020, the Centers for Disease Control and Prevention published a report about the increased adverse behavioral health conditions brought on by the pandemic.[1] In one particular month, 11 percent of those polled indicated that they had seriously considered suicide. For young adults aged eighteen to twenty-four years, that statistic rose to one in four persons who seriously thought about committing suicide.

It is not that they are Albigensians. They are, however, people struggling in desperate need, willing to sacrifice their very selves in the hope of attaining liberation, security, an answer, meaning, peace. Something More.

That Something More has a name: Jesus Christ.

However, unless there is someone at work in the world to propose that Something, unless there is someone to preach Jesus Christ in a compelling manner, the self-destructive behaviors of both the thirteenth century and the twenty-first will tragically continue.

The moment Saint Dominic encountered such catastrophic sadness, he stopped in his tracks, reordered his priorities, and changed his plans. He sat up all night with an Albigensian innkeeper, and by morning the man was converted, loving and living for Jesus Christ. Whatever Saint Dominic did in that inn needs now to be done, and done intensely.

STRUGGLE FOR SURVIVAL

From that moment on, Saint Dominic dedicated his life to winning lost souls back to Jesus Christ, especially through his preaching and the Dominican way of life he introduced to the world. Why was he so certain that his risk with the Albigensian innkeeper and the entire heretical sect was worth taking?

What may have struck Saint Dominic more than anything else was that, no matter how much the Albigensians turned their back on the Church and on conventional Christianity, they *did not give up on God*. Dominic was attentive to the religious sense driving the Albigensians to find some meaningful personal connection with the Infinite — even at the expense of their humanity. He remained confident that as long as the Albigensians persisted in looking for God, however abnormally and obliquely, he could find a way into their souls.

Maybe so, you may counter, but today atheism is rampant, fashionable, and — for many — the only sensible response to the madness. Or at least practical atheism, such as that described by Archbishop Charles J. Chaput: "In practice, American society now breeds a kind of radical self-focus and practical atheism — not by refuting faith in God, but by rendering God irrelevant to peoples' needs and urgencies of the moment."[2]

All the same, Pope Francis speaks prophetically in *Evangelii Gaudium* when he states: "Today, our challenge is not so much atheism as the need to respond adequately to many people's thirst for God, lest they try to satisfy it with alienating solutions. ... In their daily lives people must often struggle for survival, and this struggle contains within it a profound understanding of life, which often includes a deep religious sense."[3]

Saint Dominic was totally attuned to the human thirst for

God, convinced that "only something infinite will suffice for man, something that will always be more than he can ever attain."[4] He lived by the conviction that "only the God who himself became finite in order to tear open our finitude and lead us out into the wide spaces of his infinity, only he corresponds to the question of our being."[5] And that is what Dominic preached. As our Dominican priest authors observe in chapter 2: "Saint Dominic's genius consists in precisely this: he answered the Lord's invitation, responding generously to the needs of his day."

Although Saint Dominic lived in a world that had lost touch with the real, he himself was a man of consummate realism. He recognized the fact that, left to ourselves, alone and unaided, *we do not even know how to be human.* We do not really know who we are, what the meaning and purpose of our lives are, or what we must do to be ourselves. We do not know what we should base our lives on — what is worth living for and what is worth dying for. Fr. Colman O'Neill, the great Dominican sacramental theologian of the twentieth century, wrote: "The Christian's faith leads him to recognize that the project of being human is not within his own grasp. ... Recognition of this incapacity to be human is a first opening of the human heart to the need for a new divine initiative ... an act of love, triumphing over sin."[6]

Saint Dominic seized on this incapacity with the greatest gospel tenderness, mercy, and apostolic zeal — a radical, new divine initiative! He was convicted by the *veritas* that any purported reality failing to have Jesus Christ at its heart and center is no reality at all. For this reason, *faith is not optional*, because it is only in the acknowledgment of the existence of God, which faith confesses, that people can find the answer to the endless, gnawing need that the human being is (Julián Carrón).

Pope Benedict XVI expressed it this way: "This great saint, Saint Dominic, reminds us that in the heart of the Church a missionary fire must always burn. It must be a constant incentive to

make the first proclamation of the Gospel and, wherever necessary, a new evangelization. Christ, in fact, is the most precious
good that the men and women of every time and every place
have the right to know and love!"[7]

Such a stance makes Saint Dominic not an uberanthropol-
ogist but, rather, an authentic *mystic*, for "mysticism is the art of
union with reality" (Evelyn Underhill). In the words of an em-
inent Dominican historian, "To all the needs of his time or, we
might say, to every yearning of his age, Dominic seemed to find
answers."[8]

THE DOMINIC DIFFERENCE

How exactly did Saint Dominic achieve this? By living *a different
humanity* — a humanity irresistibly attractive even to Albigensians all too ready to relinquish their own.

There's a reason why, in the Dominican liturgy, the corpus
of the processional cross faces not forward but toward the priest
celebrant so that he can gaze upon the Crucified. This captures
liturgically the very substance of the Dominican charism. It is a
life intentionally fixed and focused on the cross of Jesus Christ
so as to receive from the sacrifice of the Lord's saving passion the
grace, the power, the mercy, and the love that overcome every
evil and make the impossible possible. Most people turn and run
from suffering; Dominicans unite themselves to it by faith.

All of Saint Dominic's biographers stress his acute compassion for and attention to the afflicted and those in need: the
starving people he sold his books for; the enslaved captives he
was willing to ransom himself for; the sinners he spent sleepless
nights praying for and weeping over. Blessed Jordan of Saxony,
the successor to Saint Dominic as Master General of the Order
of Preachers after Dominic's death, testifies about his mentor:
"His heart was filled with an admirable and almost incredible
desire for the salvation of all people."[9] Centuries later, the famous

Lacordaire (+1861) wanted the world to realize that "God had given Dominic a deep sorrow for sinners, for the afflicted and the miserable, whose woes Dominic enshrined in his inner sanctuary of compassion."[10]

This is what made — and makes! — Saint Dominic such a credible witness of the Gospel.

But you are most likely never going to spot a plaster statue of Dominic ensconced in your neighbor's flower garden. The kind of saintliness that Dominic modeled is very much akin to the holiness of the Holy Spirit himself, who, the *Catechism of the Catholic Church* (CCC) teaches, unveils Christ to us by "properly divine self-effacement" (687).

> Dominic's own holiness generated the Order that thrives to this day. George Bernanos explained: "[Saint Dominic] *is* the Order of Preachers, which was not formed by virtue of abstract calculations but by the unrestrained outpouring of its founder's life. ... If it were within our power to look upon God's works with a uniquely penetrating and pure vision, we would see the Order of Preachers as the very charity of Saint Dominic realized within space and time — his visible prayer, as it were."[11]

THE DOMINICAN WAY OF LIFE

This stirring book is an invitation to you to seek God with Saint Dominic, coming to know and love the Lord according to the Dominican charism — one that refuses to become obsolete. Even today, eight hundred years later, that need is great, as Pope Saint John Paul II pointed out in a 2001 message to the Order of Preachers: "We live in a time marked in its own way by a denial of the Incarnation. ... Many claim to admire Jesus and to value elements of his teaching. Yet he remains distant: he is not truly known, loved, and obeyed. ... Ours is an age which denies the Incarnation in a multitude of practical ways, and the consequences of this denial are clear and disturbing."[12]

We, too, live in a world that has lost touch with the real. Dazed and disturbed, we seek godly answers to the critical questions undergirding life: What is good? What is true? What is justice? What is love?

Let Saint Dominic draw you into the Dominican way of life: a life rooted in the Incarnation, in which every controversy churned up by the world finds an answer in God's Son become flesh; a life lived with confidence and certainty that truth is real and that happiness is attained by surrendering to *veritas;* a life that casts out the blackmail of suffering and sin by clinging in faith to Christ crucified; a life of ever-expanding Real Presence that we become through our love of the Holy Eucharist; a life of holy obedience that equips us constantly to overcome the false self in our hearts so as to live with integrity and virtue; a life that embraces the Word of God as a friend living and acting, purifying and illuminating us; a life of study that grows our knowledge and love of God through sacred learning; a life of Gospel witness lived to praise, to bless, to preach; a life of devout prayer engendering deeper intimacy with Jesus Christ and his Church; a life of beautiful community; a life lived in love with the Blessed Virgin Mary.

Saint Dominic, pray for us!

Peter John Cameron, OP
Prior, St. Patrick Priory
Columbus, Ohio

Introduction
Holiness Is Often Hidden

St. Dominic Chapel at Providence College is a positively luminous church. With simple, plain walls, the brilliant stained-glass windows shine radiantly, brightening the space on even cloudy days. It has been called "a thin place" — that is, a place where it's easy to be close to God. All beautiful churches aspire to be so. Basilicas, cathedrals, parish churches, and college chapels are places where heaven and earth meet. The careful planning and exquisite craftsmanship that produce radiant art draw weary souls up out of the mire of the here and now to be captured, if for a moment, by the things that are above.

But the saints depicted in such places, their likenesses glorified in statues and windows, can seem very far from us. St. Dominic Chapel is no exception. The windows depicting the life of Saint Dominic, the founder of the Order of Preachers, loom far above those kneeling in prayer below. This physical distance is only magnified by the historical distance of the saint's life. Most people no longer dress like him. Few practicing Catholics today know much about his life. He died eight centuries ago, in 1221, and it can be tempting to overlook the wisdom and virtue of such a man. Many might easily say: What could a medieval saint offer me for my life today?

Part of the difficulty in knowing Saint Dominic stems from the fact that our God delights in the quiet, gentle workings of grace. Holiness is often hidden. Because of this fundamental principle, many people — especially those just beginning to take the Faith seriously or just returning to its regular practice — find the spiritual life frustrating. We like to advance quickly, note our progress, and, in so doing, measure our worth. But progress in the spiritual life resists our quantitative assessments. Growth in our love of God simply does not work that way.

Jesus teaches that his kingdom — that is, his way of life — takes hold mysteriously. Against our modern impulses, the development of Christian living is more like the cultivation of the earth than the accomplishment of a degree or advancement in the workplace. In the parable of the growing seed, the Lord says: "The kingdom of God is as if a man should scatter seed upon the ground, and should sleep and rise night and day, and the seed should sprout and grow, he knows not how. The earth produces of itself, first the blade, then the ear, then the full grain in the ear" (Mk 4:26–28). The Christian way of life can be concealed and obscure. Progress in the spiritual life is often slow, modest, even unnoticed.

The saints who master this way of life are often hidden. Of course, there are counterexamples. St. John Henry Newman's collected works span thirty-one volumes! There's plenty there to examine. Pope Saint John Paul II dominated the world stage for more than twenty-five years. Saint Mother Teresa's fame is so great that her name is practically synonymous with *sancti-*

ty. Dominic is unlike these saints. Still less is he like Francis of Assisi or Teresa of Ávila or John Baptiste de La Salle or Ignatius of Loyola or Francis de Sales. He did not leave an extraordinary deposit of writings to be examined and emulated. Dominic, despite being the founder of one of the greatest movements in the Church in the Middle Ages, is a hidden sort of saint.

But it is possible to pull back the veil. After all, the saints are given to us to inspire us and to be followed. The saints became holy by offering back to God the love he first poured into their hearts. Their imitation of Christ, the beloved Son who returns to the Father in the Father's perfect love, patterns for us the way to transcend the ever-present temptation of self-love. The saints imitate Christ, and we — well, we should imitate the saints. We can, by study and prayer, come to know them more deeply and, through them, be led to greater love of God. We can piece their lives together by careful examination of their virtues, especially charity, and emulate them.

Dominic is no exception. To say that his life was hidden is not to say that we know nothing about him. We have remarkable stories preserved by Dominic's spiritual sons and daughters. In fact, the testimony offered at his canonization, which will be quoted throughout this book, presents a picture of an uncommonly compassionate and well-loved man.

Preferring God above all other things and loving the Lord with an undivided heart, Saint Dominic modeled how all of us ought to imitate Christ. Just as God was willing to take human flesh, to descend to our way of life, Dominic was willing to be changed by God's grace, by divine charity. His dedication to prayer and penance and his love of the brethren — expressed by his wise governance of his new religious order — were the deep foundation of his project of being conformed to God.

Discovering Saint Dominic's way of life is like chancing upon a hidden spring. Brushing aside the clutter and debris of the ages, it is possible now to kneel and drink from his life's waters of wisdom and be refreshed. Years after the life of Dominic, Saint Catherine of Siena (d. 1380), a woman vowed to his way of life, would write, "You are invited to the fountain of living water of grace." Catherine here refers to John's Gospel, where the Lord declares, "If any one thirst, let him come to me and drink" (7:37). Christ crucified bestows an abundance of grace, like a spring of water welling up to a great fountain, given to refresh and revive the soul.

In Catherine's *Dialogue*, we learn that the soul conformed to God is another Christ. Dominic would be so closely conformed to Christ as a priest and a preacher that it is right to think of Dominic as an *alter Christus* (another Christ). Dominic is a spring from which flows Christ's living water; his way of life pours forth a flood of heavenly graces, enabling those who adopt that way of life to flourish in a life with God.

This way of life offers a rich approach to Christian living. In the chaos of life, Saint Dominic's project helps us to order and arrange our lives. Many people today suffer from a fractured life. The struggle to harmonize professional expertise, classroom learning, hobbies, political views, family obligations, friendships, and more causes divided hearts and stagnation in believers everywhere. But Dominic's way of life is integrated. It is a life ordered by wisdom, directed toward the highest things. Every believer has to ask himself or herself: What is important to me? Will I prioritize this or that moment? This or that cause? The grace of Dominic's way of life helps us to clarify and lead.

In his day, Saint Dominic's proposal was something different. Dominic saw a need in the Church and brought to life a new and radical way of gospel living to reform the Church and save souls. He envisioned a life in which apostles of the Lord would be sent forth from their communities to be in the world, but not of it. He innovatively dispensed his brethren from many of the disciplines of the monastic religious life of his day to make them available for their chief apostolic duty of preaching. Dominic's ideas, however, were not without controversy. In his biography of the saint, Fr. Bede Jarrett, OP, notes, "Satirical writers of that and succeeding ages ... spoke of the friars as wandering tramps whose notions even of morality had been much blunted by their frequent journeyings." Despite such naysayers, Dominic wanted his preachers to be sent to the ends of the earth, ready to meet and engage the challenges and needs of his time.

In 2016, the Order of Preachers celebrated its eight hundredth anniversary. At the close of the Jubilee Mass celebrating the Order's founding, Pope Francis told a congregation of Dominican friars and sisters in Rome:

> Today, we give glory to the Father for the work that Saint Dominic carried out, full of the light and salt of Christ, 800 years ago; a work at the service of the Gospel, preached with the word and with life; a work that, with the grace of the Holy Spirit, has helped so many men and women to not be dispersed in the midst of the "carnival" of worldly curiosity, but who instead savored the taste of healthy doctrine, the taste of the Gospel and became in turn light and salt, craftsmen of good works and true brothers and sisters that glorify God and teach others to glorify God with the good works of life.

Saint Dominic offers us a way to be truly changed — as he was — by the Gospel. To bear wrongs patiently, to have a docile heart, to contemplate divine things, to love holy teaching, to thirst for justice, to hope confidently in God: this is a saintly way of acting. To follow his way of life means to become salt and light, transformed by having met Christ and lived by his grace and love.

Dominic's way of life is not simply for the men and women in the Order of Preachers — nuns, friars, active religious sisters, priestly fraternities, and laity. His response to the gratuitous gift of God is truly encouraging for all and, for that matter, is worth copying! Dominic longed to give himself over completely to the project of divine love. In the daily sacrifices of his gospel labors, he demonstrated the keys to understanding authentic friendship, discipleship, and evangelization.

Like Dominic, we must respond to God's love with love. Making present in our lives the charity of Christ is not optional. In the New Testament, love is a command, not a suggestion. But we all know that the love of the saints takes many forms. Dominic's way of life reveals the shape and nature of his love of Christ. Centuries after Dominic, we can and should adopt this form in our own lives.

Although first conceived of in the Middle Ages, Dominic's way of life is ever new. The proof is in the vibrancy of the Dominican Order today. Dominic's way of life is not a dying project. On the contrary, it is very much alive. His is a love that burns brightly still.

In this book, we will turn to the project of examining Saint Dominic's way of life. We will gaze closely at his somewhat hidden sainthood. By considering the quality of his love, it is possible to discover that this great saint is not far from us after all. We can still study his teaching, learn from him, and honor him. In so doing, our love will be purified, as was Dominic's love. Then our hearts will be bound with greater affection to God, who orders and directs all things.

Chapter 1
Living in the Word

Jesus, the source and center of faith, captured the heart of Saint Dominic and there enkindled the fires of divine love. To inquire about Dominic means to explore what it means for a person to embrace the redeeming message of Jesus Christ. For this is the heart of Dominic — a heart that burned with the fire of divine love. The promise of salvation, the teaching of the love that called forth the universe from nothing and refashions brokenness according to the designs of divine mercy: This is the message that blazed brightly in Dominic's heart.

Saint Dominic was set ablaze with the fire of this love from an early age. Some saints, such as Ignatius of Loyola and Francis of Assisi, are widely known and loved, in part, because they are famous converts. But conversion like theirs is not Dominic's story. Dominic was attracted to a life of holiness from his childhood, and he read Sacred Scripture and clung to Holy Writ throughout his life.

FELIX AND JANE: SAINT DOMINIC'S FIRST TEACHERS OF FAITH

Dominic learned the beginnings of faith from his mother, Blessed Jane of Aza, and his father, Felix, in his family's home in Caleruega, Spain. Jane was known as a compassionate woman who loved the Lord. She was a frequent pilgrim at the shrine of the monk Saint Dominic of Silos, after whom her son was named. One early biographer notes, "His father, who was called Felix, and his mother, Jane, brought the boy up religiously and were careful to have him instructed in how to read the Divine Office."[1] In learning to pray the Divine Office (the established set of psalms and readings that the daily prayer of priests and religious comprises), Dominic first studied Sacred Scripture. In an age marked by conquest, his Christian parents together handed on to their children reverential awe and tender love for God.

Pope Saint John Paul II teaches, "Parents are, through the witness of their lives, the first heralds of the Gospel for their children."[2] The pope continues, "By praying with their children, by reading the word of God with them and by introducing them deeply through Christian initiation into the Body of Christ — both the Eucharistic and the ecclesial Body — they become fully parents, in that they are begetters not only of bodily life but also of the life that through the Spirit's renewal flows from the Cross and Resurrection of Christ." This is the map for Christian family life. And, happily, it is the life of faith and family that Dominic knew.

With two older brothers who had already chosen priesthood as their life's work, one could easily understand that Dominic's father, Felix de Guzman, may have longed to see his third son soldiering, administering family lands, and carrying on the family name. Dominic's destiny, though, was to carry the book rather than the sword.

SCHOOLED IN SACRED SCRIPTURE

When it came time to begin his education, Saint Dominic was sent to study with an uncle in the village of Gumiel de Izan. The uncle, a parish priest, encouraged him in his study of the word of God. Known to be a serious and thoughtful child, Dominic is said to have excelled at his studies from a young age and to have preferred reading to games.

After seven years with his uncle, Dominic moved to Palencia, where he began his formal university studies. At Palencia, the scriptures were the bedrock of Dominic's education. Blessed Jordan of Saxony, a companion of Dominic who became the second Master General of the Order of Preachers, writes, "To these sacred studies he devoted four years, during which he learned, with such continual eagerness, to drink from the streams of Sacred Scripture that, in his untiring desire to learn, he spent his nights with almost no sleep at all and the truth which he heard made its way into the deep recesses of his mind, where it was held fast by his memory."[3]

As a student, Dominic constantly pored over Scripture, investigating commentaries and learning Scripture's meanings. A biographer attests that the wisdom of God found in the scriptures "flowed from his mind to the sanctuary of his heart, and was revealed in his actions."[4] No doubt here at Palencia he began to memorize the scriptures, or perhaps better said, to know them by heart and manifest this love by the brilliance of his chosen way of life.

For many Catholics, Scripture is dry and distant. For the average person in the pew, the Bible is not easy reading — ancient texts, cloaked in layers of meaning. But the Bible, the word of God, was not a difficult or abstract book for Saint Dominic. Fr. Paul Murray, OP, states, "For Dominic, it was not so much the experience of the Word or the taste of the Word that mattered most, but rather the Word itself, and the mission he received to *speak* the Word."[5] For Dominic, God's mercy and power leapt from the pages of Scripture, and he was impelled to share the wondrous things he read and prayed.

We have limited biographical sources about Saint Dominic, so some of the most important evidence of his holiness comes down to us from the investigations held as the Church determined whether to canonize him. (Canonization is the official procedure that declares a person a saint.) After his death, two main investigations took place during his canonization process, one in Toulouse, France, and one in Bologna, Italy. In those testimonies, witnesses repeatedly offered stories attesting to Dominic's devotion to the Bible. One witness, Brother Buonviso, testified at the proceedings, saying, "During the psalmody, tears used to flow in great abundance from his eyes."[6]

Saint Dominic wanted the brothers of his religious order to love Scripture too and to make it the bedrock of their study, as he had. We are told, "In letters and in spoken words he encouraged the brethren to apply themselves to the study of the New and Old Testaments more than to any other reading."[7] He sent them to the rising medieval universities, where they could learn and become well versed in Scripture. By knowing the word of God well, their spiritual lives would flourish, and they would be able to communicate it to all.

The reading and study of Sacred Scripture was the height of Dominic's learning. Jordan of Saxony describes Dominic as a granary, storing up the seeds of the Word of God. But Jordan is quick to tell us that Dominic did not simply store in his mind the wisdom he gained from Scripture; he lived it. One can readily apply to Dominic the great truth of the Gospel: "Blessed rather are those who hear the word of God and keep it" (Lk 11:28). For him, Scripture was not merely the object of inquiry; it was the informing principle of his life.

This abundant love for the holy word of God was made clear

throughout his life. One biographer testifies, "He always carried round with him the gospel of Matthew and the letters of Paul, and he read them so often that he knew them by heart."[8] Imagine how well worn those pages must have been! They would have been his source of consolation in times of trial and his words of gratitude amid abundant joy.

So great was Dominic's love of Scripture that he would exhort the brethren to proclaim the words of the Bible well, particularly during liturgical celebrations. We are told, "He used to encourage the brethren in choir, now on one side, now on the other, to sing well and excellently and to recite the psalms with devotion."[9] He never wanted the liturgy to become rote for his brothers, as can so easily happen after years of daily recitation. Dominic was not content for the passages of Scripture to be recited without proper care and heartfelt attention. Rather, he encouraged his brothers to experience them anew each day in the liturgy and in their practice of the Christian life.

SCRIPTURE: THE CENTER OF THE SPIRITUAL LIFE

Today, this love of Scripture permeates the order Saint Dominic founded. In fact, the constitutions of the Dominican Order admonish the friars, saying, "In all circumstances maintain intimate communication with God through a friendly union with Christ nourished by Sacred Scripture and the mystery of the Eucharist."[10] The scriptures are the center of the relationship a friar has with God. Even more vividly, the constitutions of the nuns of the Order state, "The nuns should above all keep the Sacred Scriptures at hand. They should ponder them deeply, so that like our blessed Father [Dominic], they may pass easily from reading to prayer, from prayer to meditation, and from meditation to contemplation."[11] All of Dominic's spiritual sons and daughters, not just those associated with the Order, but anyone who would readily love and embrace his example, should give Sacred Scripture pride of place in their lives.

The central role of Scripture in the spiritual life is not a unique claim of Saint Dominic. Centuries before him, the monk John Cassian, founder of several monasteries in Marseille taught, "But as our mind is increasingly renewed by this study, the face of Scripture will also begin to be renewed, and the beauty of a more sacred understanding will somehow grow with the person who is making progress."[12] Cassian's writings were some of Dominic's favorite spiritual reading, and it is this monastic love of Scripture that fired and formed Dominic and inspired his daily life.

Much more recently, the Second Vatican Council stressed that such love of Scripture should be a mainstay for all Christians:

> All the clergy must hold fast to the Sacred Scriptures through diligent sacred reading and careful study, especially the priests of Christ. ... The sacred synod also earnestly and especially urges all the Christian faithful, especially Religious, to learn by frequent reading of the divine Scriptures the "excellent knowledge of Jesus Christ" (Phil 3:8). "For ignorance of the Scriptures is ignorance of Christ" (Saint Jerome).[13]

Priests, consecrated religious, and the lay faithful are all urged to cling to the scriptures, devoutly reading them, studying them, and praying over them. Saint Dominic, then, can be our guide. The pattern of his holy life, given his profound love of Sacred Scripture, illuminates for us a path to follow. Each follower of Dominic should ask: How can I grow in my love for God through the Bible, as Dominic did?

Following his example, we should seek to be steeped in the

scriptures and should be able to converse readily about them. We should know the stories of the Bible as we know the stories of our families. In fact, Pope Francis has called for the Third Sunday of Ordinary Time to be set aside each year as the Sunday of the word of God. He teaches:

> The sweetness of God's word leads us to share it with all those whom we encounter in this life and to proclaim the sure hope that it contains (see 1 Pt 3:15–16). Its bitterness, in turn, often comes from our realization of how difficult it is to live that word consistently, or our personal experience of seeing it rejected as meaningless for life. We should never take God's word for granted, but instead let ourselves be nourished by it, in order to acknowledge and live fully our relationship with him and with our brothers and sisters.[14]

We should not shy away from the difficult teachings and questions the scriptures contain. Earnest pursuit of God will be rewarded in the study of the testimony of his love. Those who seek daily nourishment from Scripture and probe its mysteries, like Saint Dominic, will love the souls in need in front of them, driven neither by aloof scientific inquiry nor by the search for programmatic and scripted responses to life's urgent questions.

THE WORD OF GOD AT HOLY MASS

Saint Dominic considered the celebration of Holy Mass, the Eucharistic liturgy, of very great importance. It was so important to him that Brother Bonaventure of Verona testified, "When traveling he celebrated Mass almost every day if he found a church." Dominic so loved the Mass that it very frequently moved him to tears. Brother Bonaventure testifies, "When he sang Mass, he shed many tears, as the witness himself saw it happen."

In fact, many witnesses speak of Dominic's love of the Mass. Brother Buonviso's testimony states, "Sometimes the witness served his Mass. He would then watch his expression, and he used to see so many tears running down his face that the drops ran in a stream." Additionally, the testimony of Brother Frugerio of Penne includes the following: "He saw [Dominic] celebrate Mass many times, both in the monastery and on journeys, and there was not a single time when he did not shed many tears. The witness knew all this because he had seen it." Other witnesses, such as Brother Stephen and Brother Paul of Venice, say the same thing.

Surely Saint Dominic loved the Mass because he knew that Our Lord was truly present there, hidden under the guise of bread and wine. No doubt he loved the words of the Church's ancient prayers and the assembly of the brethren praying together. But certainly he also loved the Mass because the Mass is the privileged place of the proclamation of the holy word of God, which is also a making present of Christ. The Second Vatican Council reminds us, "He is present in His word, since it is He Himself who speaks when the holy scriptures are read in the Church."[15] Christ is present in the proclamation of the word: instructing, admonishing, exhorting, and healing in the scriptures.

Following the example of Saint Dominic, every Catholic can grow in his or her love of God by intentionally cultivating a desire for his word proclaimed at Mass each Sunday or even each day. When we read the scriptures before Mass and pray over them, we can hear more clearly the words that God intends to speak to us in the liturgy.

Even if we do not attend daily Mass, it's a good spiritual practice to look over each day's readings. Another method of keeping Scripture regularly in our lives is to continue to reflect on the Sunday readings throughout the week. Read all three readings from Sunday Mass each day of the week, or read one each day (first reading, second reading, Gospel) in two cycles.

THE WORD OF GOD IN THE
LITURGY OF THE HOURS

One of the principal duties of religious is to pray. This dedication to prayer marks the monastic life, and it marks the life that Dominic handed on to his brethren. Brother Ralph testifies of Saint Dominic, "Devoted to the Divine Office, he always attended choir with the community." Carrying on this tradition, each day Dominican friars and sisters gather in their chapels to sing the Divine Office, or, as the Church also calls these prayers, the Liturgy of the Hours.

This rhythm of prayer, which sets apart the different periods of the day for God, helps religious brothers and sisters to keep their minds and hearts focused on the things of heaven. The main substance of these prescribed prayers of the universal Church is Holy Scripture. The psalms and excerpts from the Old and New Testaments are set to music and, in the Dominican fashion, are sung, with Dominicans seated facing each other in choir, alternating from side to side. Thus, Dominican chapels are places where the word of God is proclaimed, brothers and sisters hearing over and over again from each other assurances of God's goodness, mercy, and love.

The Second Vatican Council teaches, "By tradition going back to early Christian times, the divine office is devised so that the whole course of the day and night is made holy by the praises of God."[16] Recognizing that not every second can be spent in the chapel in prayer (even friars and sisters have to eat, after all), the Liturgy of the Hours ensures that the day taken as a whole is consecrated, punctuated by visits to the Lord, seeing him present in his holy word.

Lay Catholics, too, can join in these rhythms of prayer. With a bit of instruction, laypeople can easily pray the Divine Office at home, consecrating the day to God. Again, the Church teaches, "All who render this service are not only fulfilling a duty of the Church, but also are sharing in the greatest honor of Christ's spouse, for by offering these praises to God they are standing before God's throne in the name of the Church their Mother."[17] Often Christians have a desire to pray, to say more to God than a memorized prayer. In the Liturgy of the Hours, the Church gives us a language in which we can pray. For those who struggle, those looking to join in the joys and sorrows of the universal Church, the liturgy provides the means.

Saint John Paul II teaches, "In singing the Psalms, the Christian feels a sort of harmony between the Spirit present in the scriptures and the Spirit who dwells within him through the grace of Baptism."[18] Dominic knew and loved that harmony of Spirit. The sorrowful laments and joyful hymns alike were his own. Receiving the inspired word of God in the sung prayer of the Church, he handed it back over to God, devoting himself to the solemn duty of prayer.

SCRIPTURE AND PRIVATE PRAYER

One report describes Saint Dominic's frequent retreat to solitude to read and pray: "Sober and alert in his mind, and anointed with a spirit of devotion which he had drawn from the divine words which had been sung in choir or in the refectory, he would quickly go and sit down in some place by himself, in a room or somewhere, to read or to pray, recollecting himself in himself and fixing himself in the presence of God. He would sit there quietly and open some book."[19]

Like Moses and the prophets who conversed with the Most High, Dominic would turn to the scriptures to hear the voice of God. In poring over the words of Sacred Scripture, he would pass from reading to prayer, and then from prayer to meditation.

Dominic's gestures showed the reverence he had while reading Scripture. A venerable Dominican tradition holds, "When he was reading like this by himself, he would do reverence to the book, bowing over it and kissing it, especially if it was a book of the gospels or if he was reading the words Christ pronounced with his own lips."[20] We should not be afraid to recognize in our posture and with signs of affection the sacred word before us. On the contrary, we should treat the very page with respect: Our Bibles should be beautiful and kept in worthy places at hand. These outward signs cultivate our interior disposition and prepare us to receive the word of God.

Like Saint Dominic, we can retire to the quiet of our own rooms and, closing the door, seek to be alone with God. God will speak to us through the page. Like Dominic, we might begin our reading of Scripture in prayer, beseeching God to send the grace we need to enlighten our minds as we read. Then we will turn readily from reading to prayer, allowing our mind to be led where Christ wishes.

Reading Scripture is not like reading a novel. Our purpose is not to pass quickly from page to page as we watch a story unfold. Our reading of the scriptures should be meditative. We should return to the same stories over and over, ruminating on them. Saint Dominic had his particular favorite books of the Bible: he loved the Gospel of Matthew and the letters of Saint Paul. In the same way, you can turn to the books of the Bible that nourish you.

Dominic also borrowed a custom from the Desert Fathers as he prayed with Scripture. The Desert Fathers had the custom of reciting little "darts" of Scripture. Picking a verse or two, they would recite them repeatedly over the course of the day. These snippets of Scripture were sharp and piercing, like darts, which they could let fly against any temptations that crossed their minds. Dominic did this as well. The brethren recounted, "Sometimes he could not contain his voice, and the brethren would hear him saying: 'To you Lord, will I cry, do not turn away from me in silence ...' and other such words from sacred scripture."[21] With these little darts of Scripture, Dominic would kneel before a crucifix and beseech the Lord.

After the fashion of Saint Dominic, anyone can choose a verse or two of Scripture to learn by heart. Pray them over and over, allowing the words to wash over you. As water polishes a stone, a phrase or two of Sacred Scripture will round the rough edges of the soul. Instead of crying out in frustration or exasperation, our crying out can be in inspired words. Like Dominic and the Desert Fathers of old, we can train ourselves to allow God's word to fall easily from our lips, raising our hearts and minds in prayer.

SEEKING HUMILITY OF HEART

Saint Dominic's study of Sacred Scripture, in the solitude of his room, did not distance him from those he loved. In fact, his love of God and his love of Scripture spurred him on to preach for the salvation of souls. His knowledge of Scripture was a living thing, shaping the compassion and mercy of his heart.

Dominic must have known and taken to heart the admonishments of John Cassian. The monk teaches, "If you wish to attain to a true knowledge of Scripture, then you must first hasten to acquire a steadfast humility of heart which will, by the perfection of love, bring you not to the knowledge which puffs up but to that which enlightens."[22] In the end, Dominic's knowledge of Scripture was a tremendous thing — not simply because of what he knew, but because what he knew fashioned his heart into the heart of a saint.

Chapter 2
Given to Truth

"The heavens are telling the glory of God; / and the firmament proclaims his handiwork," begins Psalm 19. In the scriptures, the stars signify the grandeur of God. The sun, the moon, and the great lights of the sky are fashioned and commanded by God's providential hand. They are causes of wonder, and they lift our minds to ponder the highest things. For when we see the shining stars of heaven, the glorious spectacle of the night sky, we are led to marvel at the awesome power of the God who made them.

The greatest seekers of knowledge probe the mysteries of the cosmos. Stargazers are truth seekers, searching for the answers to the deepest mysteries of the universe, for order and meaning. It is certainly appropriate that Saint Dominic, who founded an order dedicated to truth, is the patron saint of astronomers. This patronage seems to have been awarded in part owing to a story of his christening. At Dominic's baptism, his mother, Blessed Jane of Aza, saw a star descend upon his forehead. In traditional artwork, Dominic is depicted with a star at the crown of his head. The image of the star is appropriate in a deeper spiritual sense as well. Saint Dominic's mission was to give light to souls, enlightening minds by preaching the mysteries of faith. In a moving passage in her *Dialogue*, Saint Catherine of Siena shares a revelation the Lord made known to her. God the Father says to Catherine, "And look at the ship of your father Dominic, my beloved son. He governed it with a perfect rule, asking [his followers] to be attentive only to my honor and the salvation of souls with the light of learning. He wished to build his foundation on this light."[1] The science of the Order of Preachers, the light Saint Dominic bestows, is the science of wisdom. Divine truth — pursued, investigated, preached, and loved — is the object and aim of Saint Dominic's Order.

VERITAS

"What is truth?" asks Pontius Pilate in John's Gospel (see 18:38). Centuries before, the ancient Greek philosopher Aristotle (d. 322 BC) proposed a rather concise and practical definition. He wrote in his *Metaphysics* that truth means "to say of what is that it is, and of what is not that it is not."[2] For Aristotle, saying that something is true more or less means that the individual thing corresponds to reality. Commonsensical and straightforward, Aristotle says truth is simply that which is.

Centuries after Aristotle, Saint Thomas Aquinas (d. 1274), a Dominican friar and theologian, would recognize in Aristotle's thesis a profound insight harmonious with God's revelation. Aquinas defines truth by saying, "*Veritas est adaequatio rei et intellectus*" ("Truth is the equation of thing and intellect").[3] Aquinas realized that truth is a harmony between that which is (in reality) and ideas of things (in the intellect). Therefore, Aquinas said we can determine whether an idea is true by measuring whether that idea conforms to reality.

Human beings naturally desire truth. This desire is satisfied in Christ, who is at once the way to arrive at truth and truth itself. In John's Gospel, Christ says, "I am the way, the truth, and the life" (14:6). Truth is not just an abstract idea or a set of principles. Knowers of the truth adhere to the truth; Christ is the truth to which every Christian must conform. Truth is living. Truth is a person. Truth is Jesus Christ.

Ours is an age that does not value real, objective truth. In general, our modern world distrusts authority, institutions, and assertion of moral absolutes. We often hear the phrase "That is your truth; this is my truth."

In a homily after the death of Pope Saint John Paul II, then-Cardinal Joseph Ratzinger preached:

> Today, having a clear faith based on the Creed of the Church is often labeled as fundamentalism. Whereas relativism, that is, letting oneself be "tossed here and there, carried about by every wind of doctrine," seems the only attitude that can cope with modern times. We are building a dictatorship of relativism that does not recognize anything as definitive and whose ultimate goal consists solely of one's own ego and desires.[4]

To recognize something as definitive, to assert one divine goal as the aim of life: This is Christianity. To believe that we are destined for life with God and to order our lives according to this truth: This is the project of discipleship.

Saint Dominic lived for this truth from a young age. Having loved and practiced the Faith from his youth, he was a fervent, lifelong Christian. An obedient and faithful son of the Church, he found that the truth gave him freedom. The truth that shaped his life made him confident, joyful, and compassionate. Rather than simply agreeing to disagree with those who were living in error, Dominic loved the truth and loved other people enough to share the truth with them.

Thomas Aquinas and the long tradition of Dominican philosophers and theologians embrace in perfect consonance their founder's love of truth. In the fourteenth century, Louis IV of Bavaria would say, "The Order of Preachers is the Order of Truth, which it defends with equal fearlessness and freedom."[5] In the midst of a great renewal in the nineteenth century, Dominic's Order would choose officially for itself the epithet *Veritas*, the Latin word for truth.

PREACHING TRUTH
Saint Dominic revealed his love of truth in the course of a diplomatic journey with Bishop Diego of Osma. Alphonso IX, king of Castile, commissioned Bishop Diego to negotiate the marriage of his son Ferdinand to the daughter of a "Lord of the Marches." It is not known precisely which region included these marches. Historians suggest Scandinavia (Denmark or Sweden); the French marches, where Hugh de Lusignan dwelt (who would have been a helpful ally to Alphonso); or even the Italian marches, since Diego and Dominic passed through Rome on their return.[6] Regardless, the Spanish clerics found themselves traveling north from Osma and passing through the regions of Southern France.

It was during this journey that Saint Dominic began to see and be distressed by the rise of a particular false teaching that was leading people away from the truth. Jordan of Saxony reports: "When they reached Toulouse, they discovered that many of its people had for some time been heretics. Saint Dominic's heart was moved to pity at the great number of souls being so wretchedly deluded."[7] The widespread hold of this false teaching haunted Dominic. He wept and bemoaned the fact that souls were being deceived and kept from the saving truth.

Years of study had prepared Saint Dominic for the various meetings arranged by Divine Providence. He so loved those he encountered that he could not bear to see them cling to erroneous views of God. Instead, Dominic, the man who always *spoke to God or of God*, passionately presented the true, orthodox Catholic faith.

His contest with heresy, with false teaching, would become his life's work. At the end of their diplomatic mission, Bishop Diego and Dominic turned their efforts to the conversion and reconciliation of those who had strayed from the truth. Despite the little success Dominic had in that decade-long effort, he clung to the truth resolutely, unwilling to dilute or forsake it.

DEFENSE OF TRUTH

To be faithful to the truth means not to be swept away by the turns of ideological tides or the currents of news and events. Saint Dominic's genius consists in precisely this: He answered the Lord's invitation, responding generously to the needs of his day. He gave over his whole self to address the crisis of faith that he saw before him.

And what was this crisis? In Saint Dominic's day in the South of France, a parallel church had been established. Its adherents were known as Cathars (from the Greek word for "pure ones") or Albigensians (since the city of Albi was a stronghold of the sect). Catharism, or Albigensianism, was a form of dualism. It held that the body — and all material things, in fact — is evil. It was a resurgence of the Manichaeism combated by Saint Augustine in the fourth and fifth centuries, and we find echoes of this perennial unorthodoxy even in our own day.

Why was the Cathar heresy attractive? Especially considering that it was so deviant from the normative teachings of the

Church, why did people find it compelling? For one, Albigensians could readily explain the problem of evil. The sufferings and miseries of this life are caused not by the good God of the New Testament, they argue, but by the evil God of the Old Testament. In this cosmic view, the opposing forces of good and evil explain the violence and pain of life.

Moreover, Cathars were real ascetics. They believed that matter had been created by the degenerate God of the Old Testament and was therefore evil. Thus, they thought family life was sinful, since the multiplication of matter only promoted evil. Further, they rejected the sacraments of the Church, since the sacraments rely upon matter as the outward sign of an inward grace. They practiced instead only the *consolamentum*, a ritual laying on of hands by Cathar clerics, who were known as *perfecti*. Goodness was pure spirit and belonged to the God of the New Testament, who only appeared to have taken flesh and been born a man. For Albigensians, Jesus' holy Incarnation and birth were illusory, mere semblances.

Thus, Saint Dominic found himself defending and preaching the fundamentals of the Catholic faith. He explained that there was only one God, who, in mercy, created the world. The world was good, he proclaimed. This same God, Dominic insisted, became incarnate and died for the salvation of the world. Dominic taught and preached that the sacraments are the principles of God's love and grace, and that marriage and family life could be sanctifying. Dominic readily embraced a rigorous, ascetical life to demonstrate his conviction and faithfulness. In this way, he answered more adequately the problem of evil by pointing adamantly to the crucified Lord, who suffered it in his own flesh.

ALWAYS STUDY! TRUTH AS CHARISM

Saint Dominic made sacred study the focus of his purpose from the beginning. In his own debates and efforts to convert the Albigensians, he recognized the need for learned clergy. Truth was falling prey to the attacks of heretical doctrine, and few people knew enough to be able to defend the Church's true teachings. While poverty would be the hallmark of Saint Francis's order, founded around the same time as the Order of Preachers, Dominic would commence a project devoted to learning. Fr. Paul Murray, OP, says: "He [Dominic] came to realize that, in terms of apostolic strategy, it would not be wise simply to deliver moral exhortations to the people, and ignore the challenge to orthodoxy. What was needed, if the truth of God's Word was to be defended, and the Christian vision upheld, was an accurate and profound knowledge of Church teaching."[8]

The Church needed an army of well-trained theologians and philosophers capable of preaching her Gospel truths. The only way forward was a religious devotion to the intellectual life.

From the outset, Saint Dominic's Order was to be this reserve of intellectuals at the service of the Church. Fr. Bede Jarrett, OP, describes the Order's purpose, saying, "Not penance, but the very truths of the faith were to be its message and the burden of its prophecy. It was precisely the exposition of the deepest mysteries of the Kingdom of God that he meant to be the exact purpose of his own mission, and that of his children."[9]

Nowhere is this clearer than in Dominic's example in the earliest days of the Order. Taking the first six brethren along with him, he attended the lectures of Alexander de Stavensby in Toulouse.[10] Moreover, when he sent the first brethren to Paris in 1217, he commanded them to study, to preach, and to establish a convent — in that order![11]

Saint Dominic established his Order in the great centers of learning, just as the medieval university structures were rising. Those first houses of the Order were therefore erected in Paris, Madrid, Rome, and Bologna. In fact, in one charming anecdote, a nun records that as the friars moved from San Sisto to Santa

Sabina in Rome, they took with them their books. From the beginning, books have been important in the Dominican Order. They are necessary for those consecrated to the truth. One historian comments, "A student's need for books is obvious, but it is astonishing to see the place books occupy in the earliest Dominican texts."[12]

Saint Dominic's love of truth was ordered and commanded by his exceptional charity. His uncompromising devotion to the truth animated, rather than hindered, his love. A venerable Dominican tradition reports that a priest once asked Dominic which books he studied most. The tradition reports, "The man of God gave him this answer, that he studied more in the book of charity than in any other: and this choice of his was most wisely made, for it is indeed an all-instructive book."[13]

This was true of Dominic from a young age. While he was a student in Palencia, the region suffered a terrible famine; the poor were struck with plague, and many died. In the medieval era, books were expensive, much more so than in our day. Dominic, then a student who had need of books, sold his own texts, which he had "annotated by hand." He used the money from the sale of his prized possessions to buy food for those in need. Brother Stephen reports that Dominic's love of wisdom led him to declare, "I will not study on dead skins when men are dying of hunger."[14]

Saint Dominic considered study so essential to the life of the Order that John of Navarre reports that Dominic repeatedly told the brethren and encouraged them in letters to "always study!"[15] For the Dominican, the intellectual life is the way par excellence of discipleship. Fr. Antonin Sertillanges, OP, a renowned Dominican philosopher and theologian of the early twentieth century, writes, "The intellectual is not self-begotten; he is the son of the Idea, of the Truth, of the creative Word, the Life-giver immanent in His creation. When the thinker thinks rightly, he follows God step by step; he does not follow his own vain fancy."[16]

SAVING TRUTH

The life of study is not an invention dictated by the thinking person; rather, it is a call to discover and seek the Truth, who has arranged and fashioned all things.

Christ accomplished the salvation of the world by means of his sacrifice on Calvary. We are saved by the wood of Jesus' cross. For the Dominican, the wood of the desk is the wood of the cross. By the asceticism of study, we unite ourselves to Christ's once-and-for-all sacrifice. We bind ourselves to the wood of the cross by the wood of our desks. As Father Sertillanges says: "Work requires heroism just as a battle does. One's study is sometimes a trench where one has to stand firm, like a good martyr."[17] Applying ourselves to the study of sacred truth is the very means by which a Dominican shares in the redemption of mankind.

This commitment to study and to truth can and should be adopted by every faithful Catholic. To serve the truth first requires humility, for truth is not made; it is found. Pride, the first and greatest of sins, separates us from the truth. To allow oneself to be saved by the truth requires an act of submission. By study, we are not imposing order on the world; we are allowing the order God has given the world to wash over us. In sacred study, the deepest meanings of the most wondrous things wash over us, purifying us. By study and devotion to saving truth, we become aware of the workings and designs of God.

In addition to the study of Sacred Scripture, most Catholics can benefit greatly from reading the *Catechism of the Catholic Church*, papal encyclicals, books that give defenses and explanations of the Faith (apologetics), and the lives of the saints. By opening our minds to truth, we allow the light of God to illumine our intellects. Father Sertillanges writes, "Profound work consists in this: to let the truth sink into one, to be quietly submerged by it, to lose oneself in it, not to think that one is thinking, nor that one exists, nor that anything in the world exists but truth itself."[18]

This truth will free us and give us peace. Truth will save us from the lies the world tells us. Saving truth will preserve us even from the lies we tell ourselves. Devotion to the truth alone will open the way for us to discover who we really are and who we were made to be.

VERITAS ET CARITAS

Saint Thomas Aquinas teaches that "love follows knowledge." If something is not adequately known, it cannot be properly and fully loved. Without sound comprehension or understanding of something or someone, love's union of will is not possible. Saint Dominic believed this. He sought the truth with all of his mind and all of his heart. He pursued saving truth tirelessly, seeking to know all that he could, so that he might readily love.

For Saint Dominic, sacred study was no mere esoteric speculation. He studied the truth in order to hand it on to others through his preaching and teaching. As Blessed Humbert of Romans says, for the Dominican, "though a grace of preaching is strictly had by God's gift, a sensible preacher still ought to do what he can to ensure that his preaching is commendable, by carefully studying what he has to preach."[19] Handing on the truth to others is akin to healing souls. Recall Jesus' words from the Gospel: "Those who are well have no need of a physician, but those who are sick" (Mt 9:12). The wisdom of medicine is studied and shared to preserve bodily health. In like manner, yet with all the more urgency, are the words of saving truth handed on for the eternal good of souls!

Zeal for souls spurred Saint Dominic on in his preaching and teaching. He loved the truth for its own sake, for its own beauty. At the same time, this goodness is diffusive. Those who have known the goodness of Christ do not keep it to themselves, and this is the essence of the Dominican spirit, which loves to share truth. Blessed Humbert captures something of this when he writes:

> See then how necessary this task is. Without preaching the whole world would be in darkness, everything would be choked by the abundance of wickedness, a most dangerous famine would prevail universally, a plague of diseases would bring countless men to their death, cities would become desolate, the lack of the water of saving wisdom would lead to an unbearable drought, and no one on earth would be able to identify the ways that lead to salvation.[20]

Thus the Dominican love of truth: to show others the goodness of the Gospel, to introduce into the midst of the shadows the light of Christ. Scripture says, "Let him know that whoever brings back a sinner from the error of his way will save his soul from death and will cover a multitude of sins" (Jas 5:20). The mercy of sharing the truth not only saves those who need to hear it but is a balm for the sharer.

Saint Dominic's presentation of the truth was convicting because he lived what he taught. In an age when papal preachers traveled in elaborate retinues, Dominic adopted evangelical poverty as his way of life. His spirit was humble, and he was known always and everywhere as a joyful, compassionate man. Traveling from town to town on foot (often barefoot as a penance), he exemplified the ideals and teaching of Jesus by his simple life.

Saint Dominic knew that the men and women he spoke to were longing for saving truth. He believed, as did Saint John Paul II, that every person searches for direction and meaning. John Paul II describes this ineradicable human desire, saying: "No darkness of error or of sin can totally take away from man the light of God the Creator. In the depths of his heart there always remains a yearning for absolute truth and a thirst to attain full knowledge of it."[21]

There will be souls who resist or object, as there were in Saint Dominic's day. It is not a mercy to ignore them. Pope Benedict XVI exhorts us, saying: "To defend the truth, to articulate it with humility and conviction, and to bear witness to it in life are therefore exacting and indispensable forms of charity. Charity, in fact, 'rejoices in the truth' (1 Cor 13:6)."[22] Dominic engaged in disputations and debates. Confident in the power of the truth to sway and satisfy, he plunged himself into its defense and presentation.

SAINT DOMINIC'S *MAGNUM OPUS*

In the end, Dominic left no seminal work, no chef d'oeuvre attributed to him that every Dominican reads or knows. A curious thing, no doubt, for one so devoted to the truth. And yet neither did Christ himself put pen to page and compose his teachings. Contemplating this curiosity, Saint Thomas Aquinas writes:

> It was fitting that Christ should not commit His doctrine to writing. First, on account of His dignity: for the more excellent the teacher, the more excellent should be his manner of teaching. Consequently it was fitting that Christ, as the most excellent of teachers, should adopt that manner of teaching whereby His doctrine is imprinted on the hearts of His hearers; wherefore it is written (Mt 7:29) that "He was teaching them as one having power."[23]

The work of writing, after all, is ordained not to bibliographic history but to the embrace of truth in the reader's heart. In this way Saint Dominic follows the example of Our Lord, who wrote no testimony of his own.

Perhaps he simply had no time for writing. Organizing the Order and tending to the needs of the brethren would have been itself an exhaustive and consuming undertaking! Perhaps he had no liking for writing. Perhaps he preferred to be heard rather than read. Perhaps he chose not to write so that his sons and daughters might take his life's work to heart rather than studying it on a page.

Despite the lack of his definitive work, however, we gain much from studying Saint Dominic. On his deathbed, he told the brethren gathered around him: "My very dear brothers, this is what I leave to you as a possession to be held by right of inheritance by you, my children. Have charity, preserve humility, and possess voluntary poverty."[24] Dominic's legacy of study is neither a theological tome nor a critical edition. His legacy is a love of truth so complete that possession of truth alone, by means of charity, humility, and poverty, is all he left behind.

Chapter 3
Within the Fold

The Mass for Saint Dominic begins with this antiphon: "In the midst of the Church he opened his mouth, and the Lord filled him with the spirit of wisdom and understanding and clothed him in a robe of glory." Those first words, *in medio ecclesiae* (in the midst of the Church), capture one of the most important elements of Dominic's personal holiness. As one historian puts it, "Nothing could better express his vocation, primordially and essentially ecclesiastical."[1] Dominic was a man of the Church.

In the fullness of time, God sent his only Son to establish the communion of believers who would proclaim the kingdom of God at hand. The Second Vatican Council teaches:

> The Son, therefore, came, sent by the Father. It was in Him, before the foundation of the world, that the Father

chose us and predestined us to become adopted sons, for in Him it pleased the Father to reestablish all things. To carry out the will of the Father, Christ inaugurated the Kingdom of heaven on earth and revealed to us the mystery of that kingdom. By His obedience He brought about redemption.[2]

The Church is an institution unlike any other. The Church was planned by God from before time began, and we, the baptized, share in her saving mission. By our membership in the Church, a membership inaugurated at our baptism and strengthened by an abundance of grace at our confirmation, we share in this work of redemption.

God the Father so loved this plan of salvation, so loved the outpouring of divine grace and the wondrous union that it would bring about, that the early Christians (such as Saint Justin Martyr and Tertullian) taught that God created the world for the sake of the Church! This seems a very bold claim. How could they say such a thing? Saint Clement of Alexandria explains, "Just as God's will is creation and is called 'the world,' so his intention is the salvation of men, and it is called 'the Church.' "[3] Creation is indeed wonderful and marvelous for its own sake. God, the Lord of the universe, brought out of nothing all that is. And yet more wondrous still is the claim of the Gospel that God would want his creation to share in his divine life!

Recall the challenge of the Albigensians, presented in the last chapter. This dualist view rejected the goodness of creation; it follows, then, that they would also reject the Church, the means by which that first creation is redeemed. Saint Dominic, the defender of the goodness of creation, was the defender of the Church.

IN MEDIO ECCLESIAE
One legend tells of a vision that Pope Innocent III had of Saint

Dominic: "Then one night in a dream he saw the Lateran basilica about to fall in ruins; but, while he watched fearfully, Dominic, the man of God, came running from the opposite side, placed his shoulders against the tottering building, and held up the whole structure."[4]

Regardless of the strict historical veracity of the dream (early Franciscan sources report a similar vision of Saint Francis), the symbolism of the dream is telling. Dominic, man of the Church, holds up the pope's own cathedral, the Lateran Basilica in Rome. Early Dominicans saw their founder at the very heart of the Christian world, at the service of the pope.

Saint Dominic's love of Sacred Scripture and his love of saving truth formed the twin pillars that allowed him to build up the Church. Out of that love of the Church came his urge to counter the false teachings of the Albigensians. The French author Georges Bernanos reminds us, "The spawning of a heresy is always a somewhat mysterious phenomenon. When a vice in the Church reaches a certain maturity, the heresy germinates of itself, straightaway pushing out its monstrous roots. It has its root in the mystical body; it is a deviation, a perversion of its own life."[5]

A physician, who knows the body, can diagnose a disease and prescribe a remedy. Likewise, Saint Dominic's devotion to the Mystical Body of Christ — the Church — imbued him with the grace to detect an error and propose a response. Although the difficulties of our day are very different from Dominic's thirteenth century, he nevertheless offers us inspiration and example.

THE CHURCH IS ONE

Saint Dominic headed the Order he founded for just five years before his death. One historian reports, "The work he did during this time gave the Order the unity and consistency of a great, well-planned organization. Had this work not been done, the Order might have fallen to pieces after his death or remained loosely federated, poorly governed, perhaps torn by fractional strife. These months and the final touches of Dominic's hand shaped its marvelous unity. The unity has never been broken."[6] Unlike the Franciscan movement or Benedictine monasticism (which have seen various separations and schisms), the Order of Preachers has remained one integral project since its founding. Saint Dominic left the Order, in structure and sensibility, an abiding commitment to unity that mirrors the very unity of the Church.

The Greek word for "Church" is *ekklesia*, which means "assembly." When the people of God are gathered, they are assembled as one. Another meaning of *ekklesia* interprets the word as coming from the preposition *ek*, which means "out of," and the verb *kaleo*, which means "called." Thus, *ekklesia* is the group that has been "called out of" by Christ. His summons, his invitation, becomes the union of those who have answered his voice, rescuing them from a life without him.

As Our Lord tells us in the scriptures, those who belong to the sheepfold recognize the voice of the shepherd. The sheep know their shepherd, and they follow him. Jesus himself is the Good Shepherd (see Jn 10:14–15), and the Church is his flock. The flock is one, because Christ, the Good Shepherd, unites it.

To serve the Church, therefore, means to foster unity, always and everywhere. This is what Saint Dominic did throughout his life and ministry. He preached against heresy without adding to the divisions that rocked the Church in his day. He lamented that there were sheep who followed voices other than the voice of the Good Shepherd. Abbot William Peyre testifies that during his nightly vigils, Dominic prayed, "O Lord, be merciful to Thy People. What will sinners do?"[7] For Dominic, the fact that souls were straying from the Church due to sin or false teaching was not simply to be acknowledged and passed over. Those souls became the singular cause of his concern and the object of his prayer, fasting, and apostolic efforts.

In our day, too, many voices compete with the voice of the Church. Some voices rightly decry corruption, while others seem to revel in it. The Internet only amplifies the chaos. The unity of the Church is threatened by the scandals of the clergy, by those who dismiss or attack Catholic moral teaching, and by those who present themselves falsely as definitive commentators or interpreters of the Church.

Only the Church is the Church. No voice or movement can substitute for the Mystical Body of Christ. Saint Augustine teaches:

> Let us rejoice then and give thanks that we have become not only Christians, but Christ himself. Do you understand and grasp, brethren, God's grace toward us? Marvel and rejoice: we have become Christ. For if he is the head, we are the members; he and we together are the whole man. ... The fullness of Christ then is the head and the members. But what does "head and members" mean? Christ and the Church.[8]

The Church is one because of her one foundation: Jesus Christ. She is one because of her one head: Jesus Christ. She is one because there is one mediator between God and man: Jesus Christ. Jesus is the source of the unity of the Church.

Before his death and resurrection, Jesus warned his disciples of the threat of division. At the Last Supper, he prayed, "I do not pray for these only, but also for those who believe in me through their word, that they may all be one; even as you, Father, are in me, and I in you" (Jn 17:20–21). As Our Lord was about to venture forth to his death, his prayer for his closest friends was that they *be one.* The unity among his disciples comes from their union with their master. By being united to Christ, we will be more deeply united to one another.

Authentic unity is never fostered at the expense of the truth. Rather, truth serves union. Faithful Catholics should devote themselves to works that promote union rather than discord. In the news we consume and the sources we share, we should seek out voices that serve the building up of unity rather than those that foster division. Saint Dominic, the great apostle of saving truth, adopted the prayer of Christ the High Priest as his own. It is this grace that, despite periods of conflict and reform, has preserved the unity of the Dominican Order down to our present day.

THE CHURCH IS HOLY

Saint Dominic did not begin his campaign for holiness with an external campaign of ecclesial reform. His desire to encourage holiness in all the members of the Church began with the fight against sin in his own heart. Known for his nightly prayer vigils, his fasts, his penances, and his abundant compassion and charity, Dominic fought wickedness and sin. In fact, the Dominican tradition piously holds that he never committed a mortal sin.[9] His love for the Church led him to desire holiness for all. But that battle against evil began, and was consistently fought, in his own interior life.

In St. Dominic Church in Washington, DC, there is an extraordinary stained-glass window that depicts the union of Jesus and Saint Dominic. In the depiction, the two men are aligned, and between the two there is but one heart: the Sacred Heart of Jesus. Dominic's heart pulsed with a love for the Gospel, imbued as he was with Christ's love.

This is holiness. The holiness of the Church flows not from the sanctity of her individual members, but from Christ, her beloved spouse. Christ himself sanctifies the Church, loving her as his own bride. The Church's holiness is not a composite of the goodness of her clergy and members. The Church's holiness comes from Christ, her head and founder.

Without doubt, individual members of the Church are called to holiness. The character of the holiness of the Church may not be determined by the holiness of individual Christians, but holiness is to be sought (and can be had!) by all. Pope Benedict XVI says: "Holiness, the fullness of Christian life, does not consist in carrying out extraordinary enterprises but in being united with Christ, in living his mysteries, in making our own his example, his thoughts, his behavior. The measure of holiness stems from the stature that Christ achieves in us, in as much as with the power of the Holy Spirit, we model our whole life on his."[10]

Holiness is defined by our conformity to Christ. Such was the case for Saint Dominic. He so conformed his life to the Gospel that he became an *alter Christus*, another Christ.

Saint Thomas Aquinas teaches that the faithful of the Church are made holy in four ways.[11] First, they are washed clean by the blood of Christ. The Lord's sacrifice on the cross atones for our sin and reconciles us to God the Father. Second, the faithful are anointed by the Holy Spirit, and this anointing prompts us to respond to God and makes our hearts a ready dwelling place for him. Third, the Holy Trinity comes to dwell in us. By the presence of the Father, the Son, and the Holy Spirit in our hearts, we are made holy. We become, as it were, tabernacles, vessels readied for the indwelling of God. Finally, we are made holy by invoking the name of the Lord. By calling out to God, beseeching his mercy and grace, we are made like unto him.

Because of the holiness given to the Church by Christ, she is the instrument of salvation for the world. The Church makes us holy by offering to her members the means of holiness. The great truths of who God is, who we are as his sons and daughters, what happiness means, and our eternal destiny are entrusted to the Church. In turn, the Church proclaims this saving message to the world. Pope Saint Paul VI writes:

The Church is therefore holy, though having sinners in her midst, because she herself has no other life but the life of grace. If they live her life, her members are sanctified; if they move away from her life, they fall into sins and disorders that prevent the radiation of her sanctity. This is why she suffers and does penance for those offenses, of which she has the power to free her children through the blood of Christ and the gift of the Holy Spirit.[12]

Owing to this great origin of the Church's holiness — the love and mercy of Jesus — no sins of the Church's members can erase the gift of holiness. To be sure, the scandal and corruption of unfaithful Christians, particularly the clergy, mar the Church's reputation. But despite the evident hypocrisy of some, the Church still imparts saving truth. Because of the grace given by Jesus, the Church remains a font of light illuminating a dark world.

In one of the disputations that Saint Dominic and Bishop Diego of Osma participated in, the holiness of the Church was contested outright. Jordan of Saxony tells us:

Arnold Othon said that the Roman Church, defended by the bishop of Osma, is not holy, nor [is it] the spouse of Christ, but the church of the devil, [holding] the doctrine of the demons, and that it is that Babylon which, in the Apocalypse, John calls the mother of fornications and abominations, drunk with the blood of the saints and the martyrs of Jesus Christ. Its institution is neither holy nor good, nor established by the Lord Jesus Christ.[13]

Dominic knew that the Church was founded by Jesus, and that the Church communicates the Lord's teaching and his saving message to the world. If someone does not believe the Church was founded by Jesus, how could he or she believe in the Church's continued holiness? Only the Lord could inaugurate and sustain holiness, despite the deficiency and sinfulness of the faithful.

THE CHURCH IS CATHOLIC

The holiness of the Church, as we have said, comes from Christ. The holiness of the Church includes but does not consist exclusively in the sanctification of her members. But now we must ask: To whom does this vocation of holiness extend?

At the end of Matthew's Gospel, Jesus proclaims, "Go therefore and make disciples of all nations, baptizing them in the name of the Father and of the Son and of the Holy Spirit, teaching them to observe all that I have commanded you" (28:19–20). All nations. Jesus declares that all peoples throughout the world are invited to share in the salvation he offers the members of his Church. Calling them to transcend the cultural and religious boundaries they had known to that point, Jesus commissions his disciples to witness to him to the far corners of the earth.

In fact, the word *catholic* means "universal." Pope Francis teaches, "The Church is catholic because she is *universal*, she is spread abroad through every part of the world and she proclaims the Gospel to every man and to every woman. The Church is not a group of elite; she does not only concern the few. The Church has no limits; she is sent to the totality of people, to the totality of the human race."[14]

Saint Dominic carried in his heart this missionary spirit, this desire to bring all he encountered to Christ. For years he wore a beard, the sign of a missionary. He longed to travel to the ends of the earth to preach to those who had not yet heard the saving message of the Gospel.

The early brethren themselves came from a remarkable diversity of nations. When Dominic dispatched them, he spread the first groups of friars of the Order throughout Europe, rather than simply keeping them in Toulouse or even in the South of

France. Dominic's vision was for all people; his work to share the wealth of the Gospel is for every time and place.

THE CHURCH IS APOSTOLIC

When Pope Gregory IX formally declared Saint Dominic a saint, the pope told the friars who had petitioned for Dominic's canonization, "In Dominic I knew a man who lived the rule of the apostles in its totality."[15] Jesus, who founded one Church, infusing her with holiness and giving her a mission to extend throughout the world, also gave to the Church coworkers and heirs to that mission (1 Cor 3:9). Christ gave the Church apostles, and Dominic lived, as Pope Gregory says, their rule of life "in its totality."

The Church is apostolic, which means that Jesus wished to root the Church in the prayer and teaching of his closest disciples. He called them, marking them out for this special life's work. The Second Vatican Council teaches, "Christ the Lord … commissioned the Apostles to preach to all men that Gospel which is the source of all saving truth and moral teaching, and to impart to them heavenly gifts. This Gospel had been promised in former times through the prophets, and Christ himself had fulfilled it and promulgated it with His lips."[16]

These twelve apostles, the close companions of the Lord who witnessed his miracles, learned from his preaching, and loved him as his friends, are entrusted with the role of being authentic witnesses to Christ. By their preaching and example of life, the apostles handed on what they first received from Christ. In the most extraordinary way, they offered testimony by giving their lives as martyrs.

Under the guidance and direction of the Holy Spirit, the Church continues to hand on the teaching she received from these first apostles. The apostles themselves named successors, and these successors, our bishops, teach with the apostles' authority. For modern people, this claim of authority is difficult to bear. However, Pope Saint Paul VI insists:

> No, it is not pride nor arrogance nor obstinacy nor stupidity nor folly that makes us so sure of being living, genuine members of Christ's Body, the authentic heirs of His Gospel, the lawful successors of the Apostles. It is a firm faith, a joyous conviction. We hold in our possession that great heritage of truth and holiness which characterizes the Catholic Church of the present day, preserving intact the living heritage of the original apostolic tradition.[17]

Saint Dominic recognized a grain of truth in the Cathar error: The Church needed clergy to witness to the Gospel way of life. The Albigensians attracted a great many Catholics by the simple, ascetical way of life of their solemnly consecrated *perfecti*. Those Catholics may well have been indifferent to the Cathar doctrines, but they were attracted to a way of life. Dominic's Order of Preachers, then, would live a worthy way of life, declaring Gospel truth by their example.

The Catholic Church has always held that preaching is a special duty of her bishops. The Second Vatican Council teaches:

> Among the principal duties of bishops the preaching of the Gospel occupies an eminent place. For bishops are preachers of the faith, who lead new disciples to Christ, and they are authentic teachers, that is, teachers endowed with the authority of Christ, who preach to the people committed to them the faith they must believe and put into practice, and by the light of the Holy Spirit illustrate that faith.[18]

With hearts illuminated by the Holy Spirit, bishops are charged with preaching the Faith to the world. Saint Dominic, who wished to take on this ministry of preaching, would do so in close collaboration with the bishops. Dominic's own late twelfth and early thirteenth centuries saw bishops unable — for one reason or another — to carry out adequately this duty of preaching. One historian says, "This was the period when bishops were like 'dumb dogs', to use the forceful expression of Pope Innocent III, borrowed from the Prophet Isaias (59:10). Due to ignorance, perhaps, they dared not bark! The Church of that time found herself in an era of 'evil silence' (*pessima taciturnitas*)."[19]

In the midst of this silence, because of this void, other preachers sprang up, and heresy flourished. Saint Dominic began to preach not as an alternative to the bishops but as a supplement to them. He received the ecclesial mandate to carry out the mission of preaching as a co-worker rather than a substitute.

Instead of seizing the authority of a bishop to preach and teach, he invested himself as a collaborator, working within the structures and authority of the Church to further the cause of reform and the preaching of the Gospel. He did not respond in anger to a lack or failure in the Church. He worked within the proper channels, unlike the Albigensians, who established their own authorities, their own church. In this way, he is a model for all of us, whether religious or lay, of how to work with our bishops and religious leaders. When we see or hear things in the Church that frustrate or alarm us, we should, like Dominic, recommit ourselves to internal renewal.

Dominic the preacher, the faithful companion of the successors of the apostles, carried out the apostolic mission of the Church. The confidence of the Gospel took him from city to city. One historian writes, "Journeyings were a necessity of his way, and they were undertaken in the same spirit of joy as had always marked with charm his manner of serving God. The chronicles tell of his passing all over Europe, reading as he strode along the roads, talking of divine things as he toiled staff in hand to his newly rising convents, and in the lightness of his heart singing hymns and antiphons."[20]

Wide roadways and simple cattle paths were as much a home to Dominic as any four walls. His apostolic mandate impelled him near and far, seeking every lost soul.

TO THE END OF TIME

Christ did not abandon the Church in the Middle Ages, despite the wounds and blemishes the faithful suffered. Nor will Christ abandon the Church now. Jesus, always true to his word, said to Peter, "And I tell you, you are Peter, and on this rock I will build my church, and the gates of Hades shall not prevail against it" (Mt 16:18). Christ has promised that the Church will endure, and so she will!

Saint Thomas Aquinas holds that the Church is secured by two foundations: the primary foundation of Christ and the secondary foundation of the apostles. No wile of evil, no force of hell, no scheme of Satan is so great that it will wipe out the work of God in the Church. Thomas says, "The firmness of a house is evident if, when it is violently struck, it does not fall. The Church similarly can never be destroyed, neither by persecution nor by error. Indeed, the Church grew during the persecutions, and both those who persecuted her and those against whom she threatened completely failed."[21]

The one, holy, catholic, and apostolic Church is loved by Christ. Christ, the wellspring of the Church's grace, will lead her through reform and renewal. Through the ages, Jesus will raise up great saints, as he raised up Saint Dominic, calling us by his preaching to ever greater holiness and love. Dominic, and the saints who imitate him, have become a new foundation, shoring up in their own age Holy Mother Church.

Chapter 4
Mystical Union

When Saint Dominic founded the Order of Preachers in the early thirteenth century, he created an entirely new form of religious life. For centuries the Church had supported various forms of religious life, but two predominated: monastic life, in which a man removed himself from the world for the sake of prayer and labor, and the "secular," or diocesan, priesthood.

It was during this time, around the turn of the thirteenth century, that the Church experienced a new movement of the Holy Spirit and a new form of religious life emerged, known as the "mendicant" orders. These were begging orders (the word *mendicant* comes from the Latin *mendicare*, "to beg"), who took religious vows and wore religious habits like their monastic counterparts. But unlike monks, who lived apart from the world in self-sufficient communities, mendicants lived in cities and ministered in urban settings like secular priests.

Saint Dominic's novel combination of monastic life and apostolic activity was often a source of scandal to both clerics and laity who, at first glance, thought these men to be rogue and disobedient monks. Nonetheless, many great mendicant orders were founded during this time: Dominic's Order of Preachers in 1216; Saint Francis of Assisi's Order of Friars Minor in 1209; the Carmelite friars in 1247; and the Augustinian friars in 1244; among others.

BETTER TO ENLIGHTEN THAN MERELY TO SHINE

A generation after the founding of the Dominicans, in the middle of the thirteenth century, these religious orders came under great scrutiny. Within a few decades of their founding, the mendicant orders had begun to influence all areas of the Church — from the life of the laity, to monastic and religious life, to even the secular priesthood. Because of this, these mendicant religious orders were forced to defend their existence and their form of life. For the Order of Preachers, this task fell to the great Saint Thomas Aquinas.

In his *Summa Theologica* Saint Thomas writes about religious life, comparing those purely contemplative forms of life to the purely active or apostolic forms. In making an argument for Dominican life, Thomas gives expression to Saint Dominic's vision: "The work of the active life is twofold. One proceeds from the fullness of contemplation, such as teaching and preaching. ... And this work is more excellent than simple contemplation. For even as it is better to enlighten than merely to shine, so is it better to give to others the fruits of one's contemplation than merely to contemplate."[1] According to Thomas, the apostolic life of preaching flows from a life of contemplating Christ.

When Saint Dominic founded the Order of Preachers in 1216, he founded an apostolic order, one whose mission was to preach the Gospel for the salvation of souls. But Dominic knew that in order to preach the Gospel, one must first live with the Word and in the Word. Dominic believed that it was, as Thomas would later write, "better to enlighten than merely to shine." For Saint Dominic, the preacher could preach only if he first knew Christ, the one to be preached. And the way in which Dominic's friars were to come to know Christ was through a life of contemplation, a life totally dedicated to one's relationship with Christ. This was not something that Dominic commanded, but something that his sons and daughters emulated after his own example. In his little book on the beginnings of the Order, Blessed Jordan of Saxony described Dominic's nightly prayers in this way:

> It was his custom to spend so much of the night in the church that he hardly seemed to have a bed in which he rested. At night he continued his prayer and watching as long as his weak body could endure it. When sleep overcame his tired body and slackened spirit, he would rest his head, after the manner of the patriarch Jacob, upon a stone before the altar or some other place. After a brief rest, he would rouse his spirit and continue his fervent prayer.[2]

Dominic was absorbed by his desire to be with Christ, day in and day out. And his own desire for Christ spilled over into a longing to introduce others to Christ by his preaching.

Dominic was known by the brethren to spend his entire night with God in whatever church happened to be closest, praying and weeping for sinners. At times, these prayers would be so loud that he would wake the sleeping brothers. They would peer into the church and see Dominic lying prostrate on the ground before the Blessed Sacrament or an altar.

This prayer of Saint Dominic is something that was noted

both by his contemporaries and by those who came to know him only after his death. Prayer was at the center of his life because Christ was the center of his life. Dominic's prayer, however, was not rote and programmatic. Rather, it was a movement of grace and the result of a deep and intimate friendship with Christ.

The constitutions that govern the Dominican Order introduce the section on prayer in this way: "The brethren shall follow the *example* of Saint Dominic, who both at home and on the road, day and night, was diligent in the divine office and in prayer and celebrated the divine mysteries with great devotion."[3] Dominic's is the example par excellence of Dominican prayer and contemplation.

FREEDOM IN STRUCTURE

Dominic's life of prayer is what inspired the great Dominican saints and mystics, such as Saint Thomas Aquinas, Saint Catherine of Siena, Saint Rose of Lima, Blessed Henry Suso, Blessed John Tauler, and Saint Catherine de Ricci, to name just a few. The constitutions that govern Dominican life spell out certain requirements, such as the celebration of Mass, the Divine Office, private prayer, and study. But when it comes to what the individual should be doing or thinking about in these different moments, how one is supposed to approach his or her relationship with Christ, very little is said. "Since the contemplation of divine things and intimate conversation and friendship with God are to be sought not only in liturgical celebrations and in reading Scripture but also in diligent private prayer, the brethren shall zealously cultivate this type of prayer."[4] That is it.

The undefined shape of the prayer prescribed by the constitutions should not convey a lax or arbitrary approach to meditation in the Order. Rather, it is another moment to glimpse the genius of Saint Dominic and the tradition of Dominican life.

As modern Christians, we like things to be spelled out for

us. It is much easier to have a set of instructions to follow or a checklist to complete. But, in the end, if the spiritual life were to be approached in such a way, the individual would become an afterthought of sorts: the person would fade into the background of his or her relationship with Christ. We are made to be in a relationship, a friendship with the living God, which is more than just accomplishing Christian tasks.

Saint Dominic understood that a balance needs to be achieved in the contemplative life — a balance between structure and freedom, a balance achieved by virtue. For Dominic, contemplation is not arrived at by putting together the right spiritual recipe, nor does it just happen because we give it a try every so often. No, Dominic realized that the life of contemplation is a gift, an invitation to share in the divine life of God, to which we are all called. It is a response to God's grace that is offered to each of us, uniquely and particularly. This calls for perseverance and regular discipline in prayer, as is required by Dominican life, but also the freedom to dive into that prayer as men and women uniquely created and called by God.

When we begin to approach prayer and contemplation with this attitude, it may be a bit overwhelming at first. The spiritual tradition is full of terminology, from vocal prayer to mental prayer, contemplation to intercessory prayer. So it is important to stick to some basic principles and definitions.

For a Dominican, prayer can be categorized according to its three main settings. First, there is the public liturgical prayer, which includes the Mass and the Divine Office, accompanied by the Rosary. Second, there is meditation, or silent prayer. Sometimes we call this "private" prayer, but it is often done at a common time in the chapel. And for Dominicans in particular, we have our sacred study, which, though not always mystical and rarely glamorous, is part of our prayer and contemplative life. This type of structure is not reserved for the Dominican, but for every Christian. Prayer seeks to occupy the entirety of our lives: at Mass, in private prayer and devotions, in learning about the Faith, in our work, and in daily tasks. Christ calls us to be united to him in every part of our lives.

WHAT IS CONTEMPLATION?

What does it mean to contemplate? In the Dominican tradition, the answer is simple: Contemplation is nothing but the raising of the soul to God.

According to the twentieth-century French Dominican Fr. Réginald Garrigou-Lagrange, OP, the Christian tradition distinguishes three degrees of mental prayer or contemplation. "In the first degree of mental prayer are found those who have begun the spiritual life and feel a repugnance for evil and attraction for good. In the second are those who are making progress through renunciation and mortification. In the third are those who are perfectly emptied of themselves, whose purified virtues reach heroism."[5] Properly speaking, then, those who have been purified are called to contemplation.

It is important, however, to realize that this contemplative prayer is not reserved to the spiritual elite but is on offer to every Christian. Growth in the spiritual life comes about by responding to God's grace given in prayer. Over time, by frequenting the sacraments, setting time aside each day to pray, and pursuing a life of virtue, we grow in the spiritual life. These fundamentals open our souls to receive more grace and to be called more deeply into prayer with God.

The height of contemplation is not something the Christian achieves, but something that he or she is drawn into. It is a gift from God, an invitation to be with him. It is something that God bestows on those who have been made ready by Christ to enter into such a depth of friendship and union.

The whole of the Christian life is a preparation for this

union with God, which is brought to perfection in the beatific vision in heaven. We are all made for this — or, perhaps more appropriately and accurately, we are made for *him*. We are made to be with God. Created with an intellect to know and a will to love, we are made to be totally enamored with and captivated and consumed by God. This is what heaven is.

We are also extended the invitation to participate in God's life now, here on earth, with and through life's difficulties and trials. This is precisely what Christ means when he calls his disciples his friends: "No longer do I call you servants, for the servant does not know what his master is doing; but I have called you friends, for all that I have heard from my Father I have made known to you" (Jn 15:15). Friendship with God is something to be lived in all aspects of our lives, from the littlest thoughts and actions to the greatest moments. The height of this friendship, however, is not some human achievement, but *contemplation* — being drawn into God's life.

The contemplative structure and the contemplative aim of the Dominican life can be our model here. In the canonization testimonies given in 1233 in Bologna, those interviewed repeatedly noted how strictly and perfectly Saint Dominic kept his rule of life.[6] This is an important characteristic of him, not because it gives us a great example of a robotic rule follower but because Dominic knew that a life dedicated to Christ was to be pursued with everything that he was. And, by his living such a life, his friendship with God would continue to deepen.

The whole notion of a rule or a form of life is meant to create a life in which Christ is the sole pursuit. The Dominican friar spends his day in and out of the chapel, chanting the liturgy, giving hours to study at his desk, spending time with the brethren at meals and recreation, and holding to the penitential practices of the life so as to be conformed not to the things of this world but to Jesus Christ. The responsibility of all Dominicans, and of all

Christian disciples, is to live with such a spirit according to their particular state in life.

YOU CANNOT GIVE WHAT YOU DO NOT HAVE

The pursuit of Christ is the goal of every Christian, and the summit of such a pursuit is to contemplate, to behold and be with God. But in order for us to be invited into such a privileged reality, we must be made ready. The grace of the sacraments, particularly the graces we receive in the Eucharist and in the Sacrament of Penance, help prepare us. Growth in the life of virtue, which is necessarily accompanied by detachment from sin and vice, is on offer to each and every person.

This is why the Second Vatican Council boldly proclaimed, "The Lord Jesus, the divine Teacher and Model of all perfection, preached holiness of life to each and every one of His disciples of every condition. He himself stands as the author and consummator of this holiness of life: 'Be you therefore perfect, even as your heavenly Father is perfect.'"[7] For the Dominican, this is lived in the regular observance of the rule of the religious life. Yet Saint Dominic's genius is also an example for every layperson. Although we cannot force our way into contemplation, our lives can and ought to be oriented to contemplation. By our faithful attendance at Mass; by developing regular habits of prayer; by cultivating times, even short periods, of silence; by our study of Scripture and the Faith, we come to know both God and the things of God. In turn, as we come to know God more and more, we are able to love more and more.

Saint Dominic certainly is an example of a life given to Christ and a life flourishing in Christ. His contemporaries bore witness to this reality in the earliest days of the Order, and his example still inspires his sons and daughters more than eight hundred years later.

Dominic is also a powerful example of how a life ordered to contemplation and union with God changes the world. There is a maxim sometimes applied to the Christian life: You cannot give what you do not have. Of course, the end or purpose of a Christian life is heaven, but we know from the Gospels that we are also called to witness to the love of Christ not as a solitary pursuit but together. "You are the light of the world," Christ says in the Gospel of Matthew. "A city set on a hill cannot be hidden. Nor do men light a lamp and put it under a bushel, but on a stand, and it gives light to all in the house. Let your light so shine before men, that they may see your good works and give glory to your Father who is in heaven" (5:14–16).

In order to shine brightly, we must first be set on fire with the love of Christ. In order to preach the word, we must know the Word intimately and personally.

A COMMON PURSUIT

It is undeniable that prayer has a personal, private, and intimate characteristic to it. But it is not something that has to be done alone, even when we are in silence — for example, when making a holy hour with others or during the period of common meditation observed by Dominicans. Praying together is a great aid in the spiritual life — and this is something that is not reserved solely to Dominicans. It is on offer to every Christian.

Prayer within families is key to nurturing the Faith. Parish communities, with Rosary groups, Bible studies, and even social groups, are essential to a thriving spiritual life and worship. This is also why Christian community enhances our relationship with Christ. We are not meant to pursue this contemplative relationship alone or in isolation but with others, in whatever form of life we are living.

A second common thread that emerges from a life of contemplation is happiness. Throughout the history of the Order, beginning with Saint Dominic, Dominicans have always been noted for their joy, even in the midst of suffering. Happiness is at the heart of Dominican life and prayer because Christ is at the center of Dominican life and prayer. In his account of Dominic's life, Fr. Bede Jarrett, OP, describes his prayer in this way:

It is not enough to know all about [Christ]; it is further necessary to know him. Hence as a means of knowledge comes love, for … the more we love the more we shall know our friends. For this reason we find Saint Dominic deliberately developing a strong personal devotion to Christ and making his spiritual life move round that central pivot. … Prayer for [Dominic] was an energetic conversation with God, not a monologue.[8]

This contemplative union, this friendship with Christ, is the source of human happiness. Father Jarret writes further:

For Saint Dominic, then, prayer was the simple converse of the soul with God; and converse is the easier, fuller, when it is between two friends. The more, then, the mind can realize the friendship with God, which is the essence of religion, the more facile is the heart's opening of itself, for the problem of prayer is always how to make God the friend not only accepted and believed in, but part of the familiar circumstance of life.[9]

The life of contemplation is something to which each Christian man and woman is called. To be swept up in the love and life of God is what our souls long for. Recognizing this, Dominic established a way of life that sought to ascend to the heights of contemplation and union with God for the sake of preaching for the salvation of souls. This way of life, inspired by the Holy Spirit and confirmed by the Magisterium, combined monastic discipline and prayer with apostolic preaching — something that was unthinkable at the time. And just as the earliest Dominican friars caused their contemporaries to stop and wonder at this new way of living, so, too, should every Christian. As we seek the heights of contemplation, our lives ought to cause people to wonder at a love so great and so powerful.

Chapter 5
Friendship unto Heaven

Saint Dominic was a man who lived and served in the heart of the Church. Because of his great love for the Church and his devotion to the scriptures, he understood that the Church provides the place for union with Christ and with one another.

This union created by Christ reaches its climax in the Gospel of John during the Last Supper discourse, when Jesus says to his disciples:

> This is my commandment, that you love one another as I have loved you. Greater love has no man than this, that a man lay down his life for his friends. *You are my friends* if you do what I command you. No longer do I call you servants, for the servant does not know what his master is doing; but I have called you friends, for all

that I have heard from my Father I have made known to you. (15:12–15; emphasis added)

Our Christian identity is necessarily bound up with the fact that we are members of one pilgrim Church, journeying to the Father. This is not a human creation, but something established by Christ himself. Sometimes we approach the Christian life as being all about denying ourselves. It's not. It's about choosing the highest goods and ordering our lives around them. Friendship is one of the highest goods. It is the point of our living together, and it is the point of the spiritual life: to enter into Trinitarian communion through friendship with Christ.

A privilege of friendship is that friends share important things, and Saint Dominic shares with us Christ's love. We see this on display in his friendship with Bishop Diego, with the first brethren of the Order, and even with those to whom he preached. Dominic's life revolved around these deep friendships.

YOU ARE MY FRIENDS

In establishing his Church, Jesus intended to create a community of men and women set not on earthly goals but on heavenly goals — a community in which each person would become more and more himself or herself through the healing reality of grace. Through this community, each person, as an adopted son or daughter of the Father, would have access to an intimate and personal relationship with the Triune God. Even on this side of eternity, this union is a foretaste of heaven.

The beauty of this, though, is that Christ never intended for us to do this alone. As Christian men and women, we are called to pursue God *together*. We are called to a life of holiness and perfection within the context of the Church, of the Mystical Body of Christ. Sometimes, when we speak of things that would define or place terms on our lives, on who we are and what we do, we may initially feel as if this limits our freedom and autonomy. The idea that our pursuit of God and of holiness is bound up within the Church might seem constraining. But, in reality, this call is something truly powerful and ultimately freeing.

As Creator, Our Lord knows us better than we know ourselves. And one truth about the way we are made is that we are created to live, work, worship, and flourish with one another. This is true not only in a Christian context; psychological and sociological studies confirm in case after case that we are social beings and that we function best in community settings. This is even more true in living out our faith.

The Church exists to give us the grace of Christ through the sacraments, but not in isolation, not alone. The Church is also a source of support and encouragement. "For I long to see you, that I may impart to you some spiritual gift to strengthen you, that is, that we may be mutually encouraged by each other's faith, both yours and mine," Saint Paul writes (Rom 1:11–12). The Christian life requires fraternity, the reassurance of community, and, at its highest, true friendship, as Our Lord shared with his disciples. It is the foundation within the Mystical Body that frees and reassures us because our belonging is predicated not on human standards but on divine.

This fraternal confidence — that we flourish by sharing life together — is at the heart of Saint Dominic and the Dominican life. One of the hallmarks of the Dominican Order is the fraternity among the brethren. According to the Dominican constitutions, the brothers of the Order are joined together to live in unity. "We are reminded by the [Rule of Saint Augustine] that the primary reason why we are gathered together is that we may dwell together in unity, and that there may be in us one mind and one heart in God."[1]

Even more explicitly, the constitutions shape this fraternal unity: "So that each convent may be a fraternal community, everyone should accept and embrace each other as members of the same body, differing indeed in talent and work, but equal in the bond of charity and of profession."[2] Strengthened by the diversity of the brothers, they are gathered as one by the graces mediated by Saint Dominic. The fraternity and unity sought after in the Order is predicated on Dominic himself.

THE ATTRACTION OF HOLINESS

One characteristic that surfaces again and again in the accounts of Saint Dominic's life is his attitude and demeanor toward all. Blessed Jordan of Saxony describes him in this way:

> More splendid than the miracles were his sublime character and burning zeal, which indisputably proved him a true vessel of honor and grace, a vessel adorned with every precious stone. His mind always retained its usual calm, unless he was stirred by compassion and mercy; and, because a joyful heart begets a cheerful face, he manifested the peaceful harmony within his soul by his cordial manner and his pleasant countenance. ... And, while the joy which shone in his features bore witness to a clear conscience, the light of his countenance was not cast down to the ground. This cheerfulness is what enabled him so easily to win everyone's affection, for, as soon as they looked at him, they were captivated. No matter where he happened to be, whether on a journey with his companions or in the house of a stranger, or even in the presence of princes, prelates, or other dignitaries, his conversation was always edifying and abounded with allusions which would draw his hearers toward love for Christ and away from love of the world. At all times his words and his works proclaimed him a man of

the Gospel. During the day, none was more affable, none more pleasant to his brethren or associates.[3]

What stands out in Blessed Jordan's description is that Dominic's attraction and contagious personality drew people to him not for his own sake but for the sake of leading others to Christ. In recounting his experience of Saint Dominic, Paul of Venice, a Dominican priest from Bologna, testified that he "never saw [Dominic] angry, upset, or troubled, even when tired out by traveling; he never gave way to passion, but was always calm, joyful in tribulations, and patient in adversities."[4] Ralph of Faenza, another Dominican priest who knew Dominic in Bologna, recounts, "[Dominic] was always cheerful and pleasant; a comforter of the brethren, he was patient, merciful and kind."[5]

Time and again Dominic's love for Christ, for the brethren, for his religious life, and for preaching defined and gave shape to his relationships. And as his sphere of influence began to grow, it shaped the way in which his friars and sisters would live the Dominican life.

Too often the path to holiness is thought of as something austere and oppressive, something that takes away our humanity and individuality. But nothing could be further from the truth. God's grace is the source of holiness, and it is that grace that frees us from sin and brokenness and allows us to become the men and women God created us to be. And what is more, this life of holiness and freedom is eminently good and attractive. This is why people have been drawn to the saints throughout the centuries: They are examples of happiness and fulfillment. Holiness is contagious; it is compelling.

THE NECESSITY OF FRIENDSHIP

Saint Dominic understood friendship to be a necessary part of life. Christ's first disciples shared their lives together, as we read in the Acts of the Apostles (see 2:42–47). The human heart longs to be united to someone else, to be loved and appreciated, affirmed and even corrected when needed. Dominic recognized this in his life and in his relationships with his friends and brothers. And, as a founder of a religious order, he established a way of living that would support the friars and sisters in an institutional way, through the profession of vows and the stability of the convent. This would, in turn, become the locus for deep, intimate, fulfilling friendships in Christ.

Continuing Dominic's legacy, Thomas Aquinas highlights the importance of friendship in his writings. Thomas's writings are often mischaracterized as impersonal and cold. Since his scholarly writings follow the typical Scholastic form of his day, the untrained eye may miss the heartfelt and delightful moments. In his *Summa Theologica*, he discusses whether friends are needed for happiness. To answer, he considers life on earth and then in heaven. With respect to our earthly life, he answers in the affirmative: "If we speak of the happiness of this life, the happy man needs friends … that he may delight in seeing them do good; and again that he may be helped by them in his good work. For in order that man may do well, whether in the works of the active life, or in those of the contemplative life, he needs the fellowship of friends."[6]

When he considers whether friends are needed or essential in heaven, however, his answer is more qualified. Initially, he says no: "But if we speak of perfect Happiness which will be in our heavenly Fatherland, the fellowship of friends is not essential to Happiness; since man has the entire fulness of his perfection in God."[7] In the beatific vision in heaven, God perfectly satisfies every human longing. Therefore, we do not *need* friends or friendship in heaven. "But," Thomas quickly points out, "the fellowship of friends conduces to the well-being of Happiness. … Consequently, friendship is, as it were, [part and parcel] with perfect

Happiness."[8]

Saint Thomas rightly affirms that because God is God, we will not need anything else in heaven, as God will be our complete fulfillment. But because friendship is such a good and important thing to who we are as human beings, it seems most fitting that we would have our friends with us in heaven so that we may adore and rejoice in God's presence *together*.

Community life experienced in the Church, in families, and in societies offers the context in which human beings can flourish. It is here that we are able to rely on the unchanging reality that, in virtue of our common profession, baptism, which makes us members of a family, we are indeed united in a common life pursuing the same end: Jesus Christ. This belonging is a source of freedom.

But this common life in the Church (as in the Dominican Order) is not only an institutional reality. It also has an essential interpersonal dimension. The common life we lead spills over and builds into friendship — the sort of friendship that Saint Dominic embodied in his life.

Such a friendship originates in the common pursuit of Christ and of preaching the Gospel, goods that exist outside of any one person and form the way in which one lives. And this, in a sense, is also the end of friendship in our Christian life — that together, as brothers or as sisters, we arrive at that for which each of us is made: union with Christ, to worship and adore him together, with one heart and one mind.

A LIFE TOGETHER

To speak about community and friendship as something idyllic or easy or natural would be a disservice to what really is. Men and women are broken and have their wounds and crosses. Any relationship, any friendship, is predicated on mercy — God's and our own. Without mercy for one another, the community (whether a religious community or the Christian community in general) becomes a place of inhumane judgment, not of growth in virtue and perfection. Without mercy, there is no hope of growth in friendship because humanity is removed from the equation. Saint Dominic's example and his establishment of communal life in his Order do not guarantee perfect relationships — either on the institutional or on the individual level. All you have to do is ask a novice who is six months into his formation, and he will have many stories to disabuse anyone of that notion. Instead, what Dominic left us, which has been cultivated and fine-tuned throughout the centuries of Dominican living, is a context in which men and women have the freedom and confidence to live together, united by the vows, pursuing Christ, and preaching the Gospel. And, in turn, such a life creates the environment in which to pursue this perfection and holiness with friends.

The genius of Saint Dominic is that he and his friars and sisters give a real example of Christian community and friendship to all. What the Dominican life offers is not a new creation, but a re-creation, a new vision and form of living such a life. And this vision is something that can be pursued by any Christian in his or her everyday life. Each Christian is called to live in community, and the foundation of this is the family. The *Catechism of the Catholic Church* teaches:

> The Christian family constitutes a specific revelation and realization of ecclesial communion, and for this reason it can and should be called a *domestic church*. It is a community of faith, hope, and charity; it assumes singular importance in the Church, as is evident in the New Testament. ... The family is a *privileged community* called to achieve "a sharing of thought and common deliberation by the spouses as well as their eager cooperation as parents in the children's upbringing."[9]

The family should be the beginning of friendship in our lives. It is the family bond that provides each member with the protection and confidence to grow, learn, and be loved. In this, married life is of utmost importance. This indissoluble bond gives men and women the ability to live the married life in pursuit of Christ and perfection together, to grow in the greatest of friendships, as Thomas Aquinas recognizes.[10]

Of course, there are different forms and types of friendships, but everyone desires a deep, personal relationship with someone else. This sharing of life is something that exists when there is a common context, whether the family or the Church or something else. Nonetheless, it is a necessary part of our human flourishing and of our Christian life.

What is more, friendship is not restricted to one vocation or another. As Christians, authentic friendships are something that we can pursue now, no matter our state in life. Life is never on hold or elsewhere. It's here, in the present moment. Friendships help us to acknowledge that and live in that.

Saint Dominic knew this reality well. He knew that men and women, created in the image of God, were not supposed to live on their own or come to God on their own. He knew that, in order for his friars and sisters to flourish, they would need a common life lived together, rooted in mercy and a stable, unchanging, reliable life that would, then, provide the room to grow in Christ-centered friendships. This reality — to build a foundation of life that is good and stable and holy so as to pursue real, true, meaningful friendships — is something that we can all work for in our lives, our families, and our Church.

Chapter 6
Free to Love

Since the fourteenth century, it has been the custom that Dominicans chant two antiphons to conclude their prayers for the day at Compline (the Church's night prayer): first, the Salve Regina to Our Lady and then the O Lumen Ecclesiae to Saint Dominic. The O Lumen is a brief litany of Dominic's holy virtues:

O lumen ecclesiae,
Doctor veritatis
Rosa patientiae,
Ebur castitatis,
Aquam sapientiae
Propinasti gratis:
Praedicator gratiae,
Nos iunge beatis.

O light of the church,
Teacher of truth,
Rose of patience,
Ivory of chastity,
You freely poured forth
The waters of wisdom,
Preacher of grace
unite us with the blessed.

This short chant lovingly expounds Saint Dominic's greatest virtues. His life is replete with stories of his incredible preaching and wisdom, his love for Christ, and his patience with the brethren. In addition to these qualities, the canonization testimonies repeatedly comment on Dominic's unfailing chastity, earning him the title *"Ebur castitatis"* or "ivory of chastity."

Brother Paul of Venice testified, "[Dominic] was the best possible comforter of the brethren and others in trouble or temptation. [Brother Paul] knew this both because he experienced it himself and also heard the same thing from others. He also said he was patient and compassionate, sober, pious, humble, kind, and chaste."[1] Brother Bonaventure of Verona also testified to Saint Dominic's purity and virginity.[2] These are just two examples of more than a dozen mentions of Dominic's chastity and virginity in the short documents drawn from his canonization inquiries.

Why such an insistence on Saint Dominic's chastity? Why did it play such a central role when recalling his qualities of sanctity? Why have Dominican friars and sisters sung of his chastity for more than seven centuries?

There are two foundational reasons. First, our Lord Jesus Christ was pure and chaste. The whole of the Christian life is an imitation of Christ, in all that he is. The call to be perfect as our Father in heaven is perfect is real (see Mt 5:48). This is the beauty of the Incarnation — that we see how Christ lived in his humanity, and, by his grace, we are able to imitate such perfection. Recalling Saint Dominic's chastity reminds us of his conformity to Christ in body and soul.

The second reason has to do with the essence of chastity. Chastity is not about the suppression of human desires but about the correct ordering and integration of human desires. Chastity is that virtue that enables us to love to our fullest capacity. It enables us to love according to the truth of reality. In recognizing the chastity of Saint Dominic, the Church celebrates not his stoic ability to repress human sexual desire but the triumph of grace, which transforms human sexual desire — and all desires — in Christ.

So often the world, and even Christians, are confused about the nature of the human person and chastity. So, in order to better understand, it is worth examining precisely why such a quality is not only something good, but something that pertains to the virtue of a saint.

As human beings, we are composed of body and soul and also made for happiness and union with God. The ordering to happiness in God is part of what it means to be human. It includes the whole of every person, body *and* soul, which necessarily encompasses our sexuality. As human beings, we are meant to live in such a way that our passions — our desires for food, drink, and sex — are governed by our intellect and our will.

Because of original sin, this proper working of the human person has fallen out of order, and this disrupts our relationships with God and with other people. We should pursue and desire those things that are truly good, but our desires for food, drink, and sex often drive our thoughts and actions. The effect of grace, in part, is to put things aright, returning this proper ordering of the person, so that our desires for food, drink, and sex are once again governed and ruled by what is highest and most noble in us: namely, our ability to know and to love.

Rational love subsumes the natural and nonrational bodily inclinations into the moral activity of the human person, which guides him to his ultimate beatitude. Bodily instincts and desires, when deliberately enacted, cannot remain morally neutral in us. Either they contribute to our attainment of the ultimate good and are morally good, or they detract from our attainment of the ultimate good and are morally evil.

SANCTIFYING DESIRES

As men and women, we are created to share in God's life and in his unlimited happiness. This happiness is the fulfillment of every human yearning, which necessarily entails the perfection of our nature, the ultimate flourishing of human life. The whole of life needs to be oriented to the attainment of this true happiness; otherwise, all that we are and do as human beings is misguided and leads to some deficient or mistaken fulfillment.

We arrive at true fulfillment and happiness through a life of virtue in imitation of Christ. The virtues are those tools, so to speak, that, when animated by the life of grace, direct man's actions to his supernatural end of happiness and union with God. It is through these stable and perfective dispositions that we acquire mastery over our actions and become entirely free.

The virtue of chastity is that tool that allows men and women to live their sexuality in an integrated way, in a way that is governed by reason. Because the intellect is the human power that can know the truth about reality, all of our actions must be governed by right reason in order to be true and loving actions. Chastity, then, should be understood not as some sort of suppression of what is natural in men and women but as a perfection of what is natural by the aid of supernatural grace. A life of chastity is really a life of true, human love through integrated expression, rather than through unhealthy repression.

Thomas Aquinas points out that these lower desires for food, drink, and sex, when healed, transformed, and elevated by grace, and when guided by reason, contribute to our sanctification.[3] These lower desires are not things to get rid of as if they, in themselves, damage the human being. Rather, when properly ordered by sanctified reason, they make the saint a saint. This is because, as human beings composed of body and soul, what we do in our bodies affects our souls, and what we do in our souls, so to speak, affects our bodies. Therefore, it is important to train ourselves in virtue. Saint Dominic lived such a life — abstaining from meat and strong wine, walking barefoot, keeping night vigils — cooperating with God's grace, to transform his desires.

AN IMITATION OF CHRIST

One who lives a life of chastity lives in imitation of Christ. For the religious who lives the evangelical counsel of chastity, as Saint Dominic did, this takes on a special context. John Paul II writes in his apostolic exhortation on religious life:

> The *chastity* of celibates and virgins, as a manifestation of dedication to God with *an undivided heart* (see 1 Cor 7:32–34), is a reflection of the *infinite love* which links the three Divine Persons in the mysterious depths of the life of the Trinity, the love to which the Incarnate Word bears witness even to the point of giving his life, the love "poured into our hearts through the Holy Spirit" (Rom 5:5), which evokes a response of total love for God and the brethren.[4]

It is through this life of Christlike chastity that the religious is bound, in an undivided way, to Christ and witnesses as an eschatological sign — that is, a sign to all people of our ultimate destination, which is heaven. The vows that a religious like Saint

Dominic professes are a consecration now in this life and a sign of the life to come. After all, the heart of Jesus' teaching is that we live for eternity. Dominic's chastity and virginity witnessed to this eschatological dimension of our faith: There is something yet to come. Dominic's chastity also witnessed to the goodness of the body. It is not just the human soul that God declares good when he creates, as we read in the book of Genesis, but the entire human being, body and soul. Dominic's adherence to this truth is perhaps no clearer than in his earliest preaching against the Albigensian heretics in the South of France, the mission that became the foundation of the Order.

Recall that these heretics were dualists who believed in two gods, one who created the good spiritual world and the other who created the evil material world. The purpose of the Albigensian version of Christianity was to live in such a way that they could be freed of all things material, including their bodies.

Such a belief system had serious implications, both theologically and practically. Theologically, the Albigensians believed in two gods, not in the one, true God. This belief denied the goodness of God and the goodness of creation as revealed in the book of Genesis. Additionally, in denying the goodness of the material world and, therefore, the goodness of the body, the Albigensians did not believe that Christ truly had a body. Practically, because they sought to avoid any association with or proliferation of matter, the Albigensians were against reproduction and held distorted views about sexuality and marriage. They also took up extreme measures of fasting — not as a spiritual discipline, but to simply punish the body.

It was this confusion about the Faith and the human person that inspired Saint Dominic's desire to preach the Gospel. Around the turn of the thirteenth century, the Church began to send emissaries in large numbers to preach and convert these heretics. But all too often, the pomp and circumstance of these groups of monks and priests served only to strengthen the Albigensian disdain for material excess.

On their return to Osma, Bishop Diego and Saint Dominic received permission from Rome to preach the truth of the Gospel to the Albigensian heretics. By 1207, Bishop Diego was ordered to return to Osma, but Dominic remained preaching for almost a decade before the Order of Preachers was officially recognized by the Holy See in 1216. During this time, Dominic's mission of preaching was full of difficulties and failures, but it was not without its successes. In 1206, Dominic founded the first monastery of Dominican nuns, largely composed of Albigensian women who had returned to the Catholic faith.

The hallmark of Saint Dominic's preaching was the authenticity of his humanity. He lived the life of a begging friar, fasting like the Albigensians, not out of disdain for his body, but out of love and a desire to save souls. He traveled across Europe barefoot, wearing leather shoes only when in a city. He spent countless hours not just preaching to crowds but speaking with individual people, trying to win their souls for Christ. In all of this, Dominic preached the truth of Jesus Christ, who is true God and true man, who assumed a real human body in the Incarnation, who truly died on the cross, and who rose from the dead.

THE FULLNESS OF LOVE

The virtue of chastity was so alive in Saint Dominic that he was able to love each person he encountered, whether a repentant woman who became one of his nuns, one of the men who left everything to follow him in his mission of preaching, or someone who had fallen away from the Faith. Dominic's chastity was a manifestation of his dedication to God, a witness to the love of the Trinity, as John Paul II wrote, and an anticipation of our eternal destiny. And those who encountered this preacher found that his love was contagious.

Saint Dominic is not merely an example for those men and women who have been called to be Dominican friars and sisters. He is no less an example for all Christians. Every man and woman is called to live a life of chastity in conformity to Christ.

The virtues are understood to be "stable dispositions" that perfect the human person, or tools by which we are able to act. Because of this, the virtues are fixed, in that they always and everywhere lead us to the good (there is no such thing as an evil act of justice), and they are also flexible (what it means to be prudent in one circumstance might be different in another). If we rightly understand the virtue of chastity to be the means by which we are able to live true, human love, then chastity is not reserved simply for the religious but is for all.

For those who are unmarried, the heart of chastity is indeed about refraining from sexual activity. The reason for this is that it is only in the context of marriage that men and women are able to give themselves to one another completely — body and soul — in truth. Through the bond of marriage, the couple choose to give themselves to something that is bigger than either person — that is, to have their love elevated and supported by grace. Love, in the end, is not something that anyone gets to create or manipulate. Rather we enter into and are transformed by it. By God's loving design, we, as men and women, are naturally made to give ourselves in marriage, body and soul, including our sexuality.

The unmarried person is made to refrain from sexual activity outside of marriage also because, for most, being single is a preparatory time for a vocation. It is the time to grow in the virtues and in one's relationship with Christ so as to be prepared to give oneself fully in a vocation, whether marriage, religious life, or priesthood.

God offers us the grace to be saved and healed from our sin, grace that transforms and elevates each part of us. This requires time not on God's part but on ours. To think that a man can just arrive at the altar to be married and be a good husband and father without any preparation is naive. The same is true for the religious and the priest. As we already described, the virtue of chastity is that tool that enables us to truly love. It teaches us and allows us to love people as persons, desiring and willing their good, not as objects.

The virtue of chastity also applies to married couples. Remember, chastity is not about suppressing our sexuality but about living and loving as we're made to live and love. Chastity is about loving in truth. For the married couple, sex is part of that chastity, but this intimacy is properly ordered to loving each other, to loving God, and to procreating children. It is the virtue of chastity that allows for this maturity and integration in the married life.

CHARACTERISTICALLY DOMINICAN

What has been said about the virtue of chastity and the living of this virtue is not particularly Dominican. Saint Dominic did not create the virtue, nor did he invent consecrated chastity. But the Dominican tradition does offer several unique things in relation to this virtue.

The Dominican tradition, in its theology, contemplation, anthropology, and even the form of Dominican life, is built on the reality that men and women are composed of body and soul. In this, we understand that there is a proper ordering: The goods of the body are ordered to the goods of the soul, but both are good. And what is more, what we do in our bodies contributes to or detracts from our pursuit of perfection and holiness. Dominic preached this, Thomas Aquinas expounded on it, and Dominicans have sought to live it for centuries — namely, that chastity is about the integrated pursuit of Christ in body and soul.

Remember that the virtues are means, tools, to achieve an

end. The end for us all is nothing short of Jesus Christ. Chastity helps to purify our hearts so that we can be detached from the simple pleasures of the flesh and can thus love other people as people and, ultimately, can love God as God with everything that we are.

As a young man, Saint Thomas Aquinas was slated to be a Benedictine monk at the great abbey of Monte Cassino. While away from the abbey completing his studies, he met the Dominican friars and decided that he would join that order. This change did not please his family, so he was taken by his brothers at his mother's orders and kept under house arrest for a year.

During this time, his family tried many tactics to change Thomas's mind, all of which failed. As a last attempt, a prostitute was sent into Thomas's room. Rather than give in to this woman and sin against chastity, he chased her out of the room with a hot poker from the fire, traced a cross on the door, and, in a vision, was girded around the waist with a cord by two angels. It is said that he never faced temptations against chastity in his life again.

From the time of Thomas's death in 1274, many people prayed to him for the grace to live chastely. In the seventeenth century, the Angelic Warfare Confraternity was established to unite people in their prayers to Saint Thomas for chastity. For some four hundred years, men and women throughout the world have together prayed this prayer for chastity:

> Chosen lily of innocence, pure Saint Thomas,
> who kept chaste the robe of baptism
> and became an angel in the flesh after being girded by
>   two angels,
> I implore you to commend me to Jesus, the Spotless
>   Lamb,
> and to Mary, the Queen of Virgins.
> Gentle protector of my purity,

ask them that I, who wear the holy sign of your victory
    over the flesh,
may also share your purity,
and after imitating you on earth
may at last come to be crowned with you among the
    angels. Amen.

The love of other people that flows from the love of God characterizes Dominican life and is an example to all. The Dominican preaches the Gospel because of love. He preaches because he has experienced the love of God in his life, and he is unable to do anything but share that. The overflow of love into sharing is not reserved to the Dominican but is something that all Christian disciples are called to do, in ways that are particular to their state in life. We are each called to preach Christ for the sake of souls, but this is possible only when we are able to love properly, as Saint Dominic did.

Chapter 7
Mission to Witness

A fter more than a decade of preaching the truth of the Gospel against the Albigenisian heresy, Saint Dominic finally received approval and confirmation of his Order by the Holy See. In a series of three bulls (ratifying documents), Pope Honorius III gave his papal approval and blessing to Dominic and his brothers.

In the first bull, issued on December 22, 1216, Pope Honorius wrote, "In the first place, indeed, we decree that the canonical Order which is known to be established according to God and the Rule of Saint Augustine in the said Church should be inviolably preserved forever."[1]

Following the confirmation of the Order, Pope Honorius issued a second bull, on January 17, 1217, confirming the Order as one dedicated to the mission of preaching:

Moreover, since the goal, rather than the combat, grants the crown, and since, among all the virtues, only perseverance receives the offered crown for those running in the race (see 1 Cor 9:24), we call upon your charity and earnestly exhort you with the command, which we impose through these apostolic letters for the remission of your sins, that, ever more strengthened in the Lord, you strive to spread the Word of God by being insistent in season and out of season and fulfilling the work of the evangelist in a praiseworthy manner.[2]

Finally, in a third bull, issued on February 11, 1217, Saint Dominic's Order received its official name, *Ordo Praedicatorum*, or Order of Friars Preachers. (This is why Dominicans include the initials "OP" after their names.) Pope Honorius famously wrote:

Therefore, we ask your allegiance and, commanding you by apostolic letters, strongly urge that, with us, you encourage in their praiseworthy design the friars of the Order of Preachers (whose salutary ministry and religious institute we believe to be pleasing to God) and regard them, out of reverence for us and the Apostolic See, as approved. Assist in their needs these men who, faithfully preaching the word of the Lord without recompense, and imitating the Lord himself alone in seeking the good of souls, have given their preference to the title of poverty.[3]

In a sense, with the approval of his Order, Saint Dominic had accomplished his mission at this point. He had dedicated his life to preaching the Gospel, not simply as a personal project, but at the service of the Church and inspired by the Holy Spirit. He created a way of living, one founded on contemplation and fraternity, study and discipline, that led to friendship and union with Christ and overflowed into preaching the Gospel. After the Order's official approbation at the end of 1216, Dominic would labor for only five more years before his death on August 6, 1221.

FOR THE SALVATION OF SOULS

Even before Saint Dominic's birth, there seem to have been indications of his preaching and establishing a religious order. There are numerous stories about the charity of Blessed Jane, Dominic's mother, but perhaps the most famous story from her life is a dream that she had about her son before he was born. Blessed Jordan of Saxony reported the dream in his book about the beginnings of the Order:

> Before his mother conceived him, she saw in a vision that she would bear in her womb a dog who, with a burning torch in his mouth and leaping from her womb, seemed to set the whole earth on fire. This was to signify that her child would be an eminent preacher who, by "barking" sacred knowledge, would rouse to vigilance souls drowsy with sin, as well as scatter throughout the world the fire which the Lord Jesus Christ came to cast upon the earth.[4]

This dream was, of course, a prophecy of Saint Dominic and his religious order dedicated to preaching. It also led to Dominic's iconography, as he is often pictured with a dog sitting at his feet, holding a burning torch in its mouth.

As we have said, Dominic was inspired to found a preaching order when he encountered the Albigensian heresy. He spent years in the South of France, preaching to the heretics, attempting to bring them back to the true Faith. One of these moments has come to define Dominic's preaching:

> When they reached Toulouse, they discovered that many
> of its people had for some time been heretics. Dominic's
> heart was moved to pity at the great number of souls be-
> ing so wretchedly deluded. At the inn where they found
> shelter in Toulouse, Dominic spent the entire night fer-
> vently exhorting and zealously arguing with the hereti-
> cal innkeeper, who, no longer able to resist the wisdom
> and the spirit that spoke, returned by God's grace to the
> true faith.[5]

The story of the innkeeper defines Dominican preaching in two
ways. First, it underlines Saint Dominic's pity for those who are
in error. His response to the heretical innkeeper was not conde-
scending or scolding but arose from his friendship with Christ
and his desire for others to have such a relationship. Second,
this story demonstrates Dominic's unmistakable perseverance.
He stayed up all night with the innkeeper not to win a specula-
tive argument or claim the moral high ground but to recover the
innkeeper's soul for Christ. One can only imagine that it was not
simply the words Dominic spoke that converted the innkeeper,
but also his witness to the Word.

These qualities are evident in another of his preaching en-
counters. In Toulouse, France, there was an Albigensian heretic,
Raymond de Grossi, who had obstinately refused to return to
the Catholic Faith. All attempts to reconcile him to the Church
failed, and he was turned over to the state to be punished. Saint
Dominic was preaching in the city at that time, and, looking at
Raymond, he told the court officials to release him. It is record-
ed that Dominic saw "the ray of divine predestination in him."
Upon Raymond's release, Dominic approached him and said, "I
know, my son, I know that, although late, you will yet be a good,
holy man."

For twenty more years, Raymond remained in his heresy, but

after that time, he returned to the Faith and became a Dominican friar.[6] This incident adds another dimension to Saint Dominic's preaching: It was efficacious. This is true of any preaching or witness to the Gospel that is inspired by the Holy Spirit. The grace of preaching disposes the soul to conversion. The timeline of conversion may not be as one might hope, but God will have his way in the end. Dominic spent his life traveling throughout Europe, preaching the Gospel, often with little immediate success. Brother Raymond did not convert until after Dominic's death. Yet his story reveals that the words we preach do change lives and convert souls.

This is always a grace. It is not the preacher who is the sole or primary cause of conversion or salvation. Rather, he is an instrument of God's revelation. Neither is it the preacher's business to know the effects or fruits of his preaching — at least not in this life. Rather, knowing that his preaching is a grace frees the preacher to be wholly focused on the work of preaching as a work of God, not of his own doing. Converting and saving souls is the work of God. Yet God chooses preachers, as Saint Paul explains (see Rom 10:14–15), to participate in this work and to serve as his instruments of salvation.

A VOCATION TO PREACH

We live in a time in the Church when preaching is quite prevalent and regular. It would be strange to go to Mass and not hear a homily. We also find many people speaking about Christ and the Gospel in different forms and from varieties of sources. So what is special about Dominican preaching? What is special about having a religious order whose charism and end are preaching, when so many others seem to be able to do the same thing?

Preaching in the Church pertains to the office of the bishop, as our bishops are the successors of the apostles. It is the bishop's job to preach the Gospel in his diocese. A priest, in virtue of his ordination, is configured to Christ and "consecrated to preach the Gospel." However, this preaching, and all that the priest does, is dependent on the bishop's apostolic power.

This was not always the case in the Church, however. In the early Church and into the Middle Ages, priests rarely, if ever, preached. This was due to a number of factors, not least of which was that priests were generally poorly educated. Homilies were not preached at Mass; in fact, it was comparatively rare for the laity to hear preaching. Saint Dominic sought to remedy this by establishing an order of preachers. When Pope Honorius established Dominic's Order as one dedicated to preaching, the friars were given universal permission to preach. That meant a Dominican friar could preach anywhere and was not limited to a specific diocese or bishop.

This historical novelty, ratified by the Holy See, gives context to the Order's charism of preaching. It is the Order of Preachers, and this order alone, that has received this mission and gift of preaching in the Church. There is no other.

This does not mean that non-Dominican priests cannot preach or that they cannot preach extremely well (history certainly proves that), but it does mean that a special grace of preaching belongs to Saint Dominic and his sons. There is a grace that the friars preachers can rely on in virtue of their profession when they preach. Because it is the Order's mission, it is brought to fruition by the Holy Spirit.

Everything that Dominicans do is aimed at preaching the Gospel. Our lives of contemplation and study, our living together in community, our penances and disciplines: all of it is aimed at the one end of preaching. This is the genius of Saint Dominic. He understood that in order to preach the Gospel, one first had to know Christ intimately and the truths of the Faith deeply, so as to bring Christ and the Faith to the world through preaching.

Even the evangelical counsels of poverty, chastity, and obedience are lived in the Dominican context in service of the preaching of the Gospel. Poverty frees the Dominican from material things and also frees him to move freely and preach where he is sent. Chastity heals concupiscence and sets aside the anxieties of family life so that the Dominican can be totally dedicated to Christ and those to whom he preaches. Obedience detaches the Dominican will from anything but the obedience of faith in service of study, prayer, and preaching. In sum, preaching is not merely something that Saint Dominic did; it is something that a Dominican cultivates at every level. Dominic lived the life of a preacher. In the same way, all Dominicans are meant to live the life of a preacher. It is an identity and a way of life.

Blessed Humbert of Romans, the fifth master of the Order of Preachers, wrote a treatise on preaching, noting that to be a preacher is indeed a vocation and a gift from God, and it necessarily requires the full cooperation of the preacher to preach well. "About the first point, observe that, granted the grace of preaching well is a special gift of God, nevertheless it demands from the preacher full application to the study of whatever is needed for the proper execution of his office."[7] Preaching is more than a simple mastery of technique; it is an overflow of his contemplation.

Preaching, then, is not simply some trade that one works on so as to be skilled; it is not a task that one takes upon himself. Rather, preaching is a grace, a gift, a call from God. It is God's work in which one participates according to his or her vocation.

THE CHARISM OF PREACHING

Fr. Humbert Clerissac, OP, explains the dynamism of Dominican preaching: "These are the three spiritual dimensions: the life of the mind in study, the absorption in God by prayer and contemplation, and the outflow of the soul into apostolic action. These three are neither mutually exclusive nor contradictory: they are the height, breadth, and depth of the soul's life."[8] The height, breadth, and depth of which Father Clerissac speaks is conveyed in the content of what is preached.

One of the mottos of the Order of Preachers is *veritas*, or truth, and this dedication and insistence on the truth is fundamental to Dominican preaching. The commitment to truth is not simply a focus on being correct, or just preaching truth claims about the Faith, but is about preaching Truth himself. This is based on the fact that our hearts follow our intellects, so the more that we know something or someone, the better we are able to love.

Clarity and truth are essential to preaching in order to help men and women come to know who God is and so love him all the more. And this is the crux of conversion. Hearing the truth preached is supposed to dispose a person to receive the graces that are on offer. This is the entire premise of Saint Dominic's founding mission in preaching to the Albigensians: that the truth of Jesus Christ and the truth of the human person are necessary for the salvation of souls. This is also why Dominic, within a year of the Order's founding, sent his brothers out in pairs and small groups to the university cities of Europe: first, so that they could be educated in truth and, second, so that they could preach the truth in these places.

Preaching the truth is not simply listing dogmatic statements or reciting doctrinal teachings. It won't suffice to mail people catechisms. Rather, the Dominican preaches truth by presenting and shedding light upon the mysteries of Christ's life. Special attention is given to the consideration of *who* Christ is in himself: Christ as the Son of God, as the God-man, as the Messiah and Savior, and so on. So much of our faith is about coming to know who God is in himself, simply for the sake of knowing him. And we do this by meditating on those things that are revealed to us in the scriptures.

An absolutely necessary corollary to the preaching of the mysteries of our faith and considering them in themselves is understanding what they teach us about us. Everything that Christ does in his life reveals the Father. He tells us, "All things have been delivered to me by my Father; and no one knows the Son except the Father, and no one knows the Father except the Son and any one to whom the Son chooses to reveal him" (Mt 11:27). He says also, "If you had known me, you would have known my Father also; henceforth you know him and have seen him" (Jn 14:7). As the Second Vatican Council reiterates: "Christ, the final Adam, by the revelation of the mystery of the Father and His love, fully reveals man to man himself and makes his supreme calling clear."[9] The closer we grow to Christ, the deeper our conversion, the better we are able to know ourselves as sinners redeemed by Christ.

This knowledge of who we are as men and women brings us to another characteristic of Dominican preaching, namely, that it seeks to address the whole human, body and soul. So often, preaching devolves into simple moral exhortation (more on this in the next and final point) or pious niceties. Neither takes into account the whole of the human person. The Incarnation, and a proper understanding of the human person in relation to the Incarnation, is the very foundation of Dominican preaching. This was precisely what Saint Dominic preached for years when combating the Albigensian heresy. Christ became man, taking a real human body and soul, in order to redeem us entirely, in our real human bodies and souls.

Finally, Dominican preaching is completely allergic to moralistic preaching — that is, preaching that boils down the Faith to a list of dos and don'ts. Of course, there are good things and evil things, and we should do the good and avoid the evil. Moral rules, however, are not the entirety or even the basis of the Christian life. Christians live as Christians because they have been moved by the grace of Christ and have come to know him, and this relationship shapes the way in which we live.

Fr. Peter John Cameron, OP, explains that the Christian life "is a relationship that springs from the acknowledgment of a Presence in my life that is the answer to my life."[10] Acting or living contrary to the teachings of our faith means acting or living contrary to the reality of Christ. The height of the moral life is not accomplishing a task list of good things but growing and striving for perfection in virtue in imitation and conformity to Christ. A life of virtue, aided by grace, transforms us inwardly so that we may live in union with God.

A UNIVERSAL MISSION

Preaching, in the strict sense, is a clerical act that has come from the apostles. The apostles, and the bishops who succeeded them, were entrusted with the spreading of the Gospel. And in virtue of their ordination, priests are given a share in this apostolic preaching.

The preaching of Saint Dominic's sons takes on a different reality because, as said above, preaching is not simply something that Dominicans do; it is who they are. The whole of the Dominican life is ordered to this mission of preaching for the salvation of souls. Nonetheless, all Dominicans, in virtue of their consecration, participate in the preaching mission of the Order. This includes the cooperator (lay) brothers, the cloistered nuns, the sisters, and the laity, each according to his or her Dominican vocation. This is not some modern idea but is from the mind of Dominic himself. In fact, Dominican nuns were established in 1206, ten years before the friars' official founding in 1216. And from the very beginning to this day, the nuns were to pray and give their lives for the preaching of the Gospel.

The way of life Saint Dominic established offers the school of preparation: to pray regularly, to study the Faith, and to do that with others. It is that simple. Dominic also shows us how to preach: to preach the truth in love and patience and to preach Christ and his mysteries, always with regard for the whole person, in pursuit of a life of virtue and happiness.

Blessed Reginald of Orleans, one of Saint Dominic's closest companions, sums up this life of preaching. After being asked if he ever regretted taking the Dominican habit, he responded, "I very much doubt if there is any merit in it for me, because I have always found so much pleasure in the Order!"[11] Despite whatever trials and setbacks, whatever failures and successes, the preaching mission is a joy that gives to life its truest meanings and its deepest satisfactions.

Similar things could be said about the other ranks of Dominicans, each contributing its own saints to the ranks of heaven. These include Saint Martin de Porres, a lay brother who lived Gospel charity among the least in society; Saint Margaret of Hungary, a nun whose prayer and penance sustained the preaching mission; Saint Catherine of Siena, a sister who proclaimed the truth and the necessity of unity in the Church; and Blessed Pier Giorgio Frassati, a lay Dominican whose love for Christ spilled into his everyday life.

This way of living is not limited to those who are formally incorporated in the Order of Preachers. The command at the end of the Gospel of Matthew is for us all: "Go therefore and make disciples of all nations" (28:19). All of us, in virtue of our baptism, are called to preach Jesus Christ in our homes, workplaces, social circles — everywhere, in fact. We're not supposed to get on a soapbox but, rather, are to testify by the very witness of our lives. In this important task, Saint Dominic is our great model and intercessor.

Chapter 8
Under the Virgin's Mantle

Since the Order's earliest days, Saint Dominic's brethren have professed an abiding devotion to the Virgin Mary. This devotion of the early friars was fostered by Dominic himself. Popes and theologians alike through the centuries have attributed the Order's early success in the mission of preaching to the intercession of the Virgin Mary. Pope Saint Pius V — a Dominican friar and renowned promoter of the Holy Rosary — writes:

> The inspired Blessed founder of the Order of Friars Preachers ... raised his eyes up unto heaven, unto that mountain of the Glorious Virgin Mary, loving Mother of God. For she by her seed has crushed the head of the twisted serpent, and has alone destroyed all heresies, and by the blessed fruit of her womb has saved a world condemned by the fall of our first parent. From her, without

human hand, was that stone cut, which, struck by wood, poured forth the abundantly flowing waters of graces.[1]

By her loving obedience — saying to the angel, "Let it be to me according to your word" (Lk 1:38) — the Virgin Mary unknotted the tangled web of our first parents' disobedience. She became the first disciple, the first to hear the promise of salvation, and devoted her heart completely to the mysteries of Christ. This life of obedience to Christ and service to his Gospel is the life of the friar preacher, as established by Saint Dominic.

Each year on May 8, the Order of Preachers worldwide turns to the Blessed Virgin Mary. On the feast of her patronage of the Order, Dominicans pray, "Virgin Mother Mary, with trust we approach you. We, your preachers, fly to you who believed in the words sent from heaven and pondered them in your heart. We stand close around you, who are always present to the gathering of apostles."

THE BLESSED VIRGIN MARY'S ORDER

The Dominican tradition attributes the foundation of the Order to the intercession of the Blessed Virgin Mary. A certain Cistercian monk, so the story goes, had spent three days and three nights in ecstasy. During that time, he witnessed the Virgin Mary beseeching her Son on behalf of sinners. With clasped hands, on bended knee, the Blessed Mother begged Christ to intervene, since many souls were being lost. The visionary reports that on the third day, yielding to her entreaties, Jesus said to Mary, "I know, sweet Mother, that sinners are being lost for want of preachers, having none to break to them the bread of the holy Scriptures, or teach the truth, or open the books now sealed to them. Wherefore, yielding to thy entreaties, I will send them new messengers, an Order of Preachers, who shall call the people and lead them to everlasting joys."[2]

Confident in the care and protection of the Blessed Mother, the early Dominicans fearlessly set out to do something new. In fact, they so loved the Virgin Mary that it was important to them to place all of their efforts under her intercession.

From the beginning, Our Lady's patronage has defended the Order against detractors. After all, Saint Dominic's project was novel, and it attracted the criticism of no small number of naysayers. Brother Walter of Trier reports a story about a holy hermitess of Saxony who had heard of the new Order of Preachers and, interested by its name, wanted to meet friars of the Order. When the woman had occasion to meet two of the brethren, she was disappointed by their youth. She lamented that the duty of preaching the Holy Word of God had fallen to unqualified children such as those friars! Later on, Our Lady appeared to the disillusioned woman and, drawing back her cloak, revealed underneath friars of the Order. On another occasion, the Virgin Mary dictated a homily to a struggling preacher. On another, she held a book while a friar preached. In these and other visions reported by the medieval Dominicans, Our Lady claimed to be protectress of the friars, guiding and directing their way.

The Virgin Mary's prayers are the very lifeblood of the preaching apostolate and are viewed as the cause of its success. Because of her intercession, the friars could be sent out into the world without fearing that they would be lost to worldliness. In one polemical tract, in an effort to defend the nature and ideals of the Order against cynics and critics, Thomas of Cantimpré writes, "Let our evil-mouthed and impious detractors beware of going against the patronage of the Mother of Christ by persecuting her children; if they do, they are liable to incur her anger, because she supports and defends her children."[3]

Though their devotion to the Blessed Virgin was by no means unique — many religious orders of the Middle Ages have similar accounts and expressions of piety — the early Dominican brethren were greatly devoted to Our Lady. For this reason, the Order would come to honor her (in the seventeenth century) with a title connecting her to their life's work: Queen of Preachers.

THE *SEIGNADOU*

On the evening of July 22, 1206, the feast of Saint Mary Magdalene, Saint Dominic sat just beyond the village of Fanjeaux, France, reading about the Apostle to the Apostles. Meditating on the life of Mary Magdalene, Dominic then turned to Our Lady, asking for a sign to confirm his project of preaching.

A fiery blaze appeared in the sky, something like a comet or a shooting star, and passed Saint Dominic overhead. Before disappearing, the star hovered over the church in Prouille. As the tradition holds, Dominic returned to the place twice more, seeing each night the same sign from heaven. On three successive nights, the Virgin Mary is purported to have sent Dominic a celestial indication of her blessing.

The word *Seignadou* means "sign from God" in the local language of that place and time. One Dominican historian notes, "The name of *Seignadou* (*Signatorium*) given to the place at least since the fifteenth century and the presence there of a cross and a chapel recall this tradition. Whatever its cause and origin may be, it does commemorate a profound reality — the certainty acquired by Saint Dominic as he stood on this promontory that it was in these parts that he had to respond to the call."[4]

Bishop Fulk of Toulouse would entrust Saint Dominic with a church and a parcel of land at Prouille. In this village, Dominic gathered the first converts from his preaching and formed them into a monastery of contemplative nuns. Their monastery — the first house of the holy preaching and Dominic's original mission station — was named Notre-Dame-de-Prouille and placed under Our Lady's protection.

THE HABIT FROM OUR LADY

One of the most distinctive aspects of the Order's tradition is the Dominican habit. As a canon, Saint Dominic wore a white tunic with a surplice, looking much like an altar server clad all in white would look at Mass. The early friars adopted the same dress. But the habit was changed, our tradition holds, by the Virgin Mary herself.

Reginald of Orleans, a renowned professor of canon law — who had taught in Paris for some time to great acclaim — fell grievously ill while visiting Rome. Saint Dominic visited him many times during his illness and persuaded him to adopt the Order's evangelical way of life in imitation of Christ. Later, the Virgin Mary appeared to Reginald and anointed his eyes, nose, ears, mouth, chest, hands, and feet in preparation for his new mission of announcing the Gospel. Jordan of Saxony relates, "Then she showed him the complete habit of this Order. At once he became well and so sudden was his cure that the physicians, who had almost given up all hope, were at a loss to explain his evident recovery."[5]

Our tradition holds that the part of the habit revealed to Reginald was a scapular. According to Blessed Jordan, Saint Dominic himself told the story of the vision and the miracle (Jordan heard Dominic relate it once in the course of a meeting in Paris). Thereafter friars adopted the custom of wearing a long white scapular rather than a surplice.

Why a scapular? The word itself is rooted in the Latin word *scapula*, which means "shoulder." In the monastic tradition, it symbolizes the yoke of Christ, and quite a few other monastic orders wear it with that understanding. But for Dominicans, the scapular is a sign of devotion to Our Lady, since she herself has given it. One historian notes, "Dominican tradition has always held that the Virgin Mother of God herself deigned to design the habit composed of light and shadow, having the brethren give up the canon's surplice which they had worn until then, and replacing it with scapular."[6]

Friars, nuns, and sisters to this day are distinguishable by their long white scapulars and black capes. Others devoted to the Order have adopted the practice of wearing a white devotional scapular. Similar to the popular brown scapular of Carmel, the white Dominican scapular is typically two white panels, joined by a cord or ribbon. The American parish priest Blessed Michael McGivney, founder of the Knights of Columbus, was entombed wearing one such white scapular, no doubt a sign of his friendship with the Order of Preachers and his devotion to Saint Dominic and the Blessed Virgin Mary.

THE SALVE REGINA

One of the greatest expressions of devotion to Our Lady is the treasury of Catholic hymns written in her honor. During his many travels, which he accomplished on foot, Saint Dominic was known to sing as he walked, and one of his favorite hymns to sing was the *Ave Maris Stella*. The first verse of that hymn sings:

> Hail, star of the sea,
> Nurturing Mother of God,
> And ever Virgin,
> Happy gate of Heaven.

Medievals used the name *Stella Maris* (Star of the Sea) as another name for the North Star. As Polaris guides seafarers safely home, so the Virgin Mary directs the way of our earthly pilgrimage. Saint Dominic, itinerant preacher and pilgrim, saw Our Lady as the guide of his journeys.

In much the same spirit, the early Dominicans adopted a custom of singing to the Virgin Mary a hymn that endures to the present day. During a time of trial at the priory in Bologna in

1230, the brethren adopted the Cistercian custom of singing the Salve Regina at the end of Compline (night prayer). Jordan of Saxony writes, "How many tears of devotion have sprung from this holy praise of God's venerable Mother? How many hearts of those who sang or listened has it not melted, how often has it not softened bitterness and installed fervor in its place? Do we believe that the Mother of our Redeemer is pleased with such praises and moved by such cries?"[7]

From Bologna the custom took hold and, by 1250, became the universal practice of the Order. The Order would adopt its own haunting melody of this traditional prayer, and the sweet pleas for the Virgin's protection would ring in Dominican convents not only in the evening of the day but in the evening of life: the hour of death.

In Dominican houses, the singing of the Salve is accompanied by the sprinkling of holy water. Another story from the early brethren recounts how a friar saw a vision of a woman passing through the dormitory, covering the friars with holy water as she passed by. The friar stopped the woman, who revealed to him, "I am Mary, the virgin Mother of Jesus, and I am come once more to visit my brethren. I bear a very special love for this Order, and what pleases me most is that you begin all your undertakings, all that you say or do during the day, by asking my help and blessing, and you likewise end them to my praise."[8]

This custom of beginning and ending each day with prayer to the Virgin Mary can be enormously profitable for any Catholic. Keep holy water at your bedside and cross yourself with it while reciting your evening prayers. Pray a simple prayer such as the Hail Mary or the Salve Regina, thereby imitating those in the Order who entrust their days to Our Lady's care.

OFFICE OF THE BLESSED VIRGIN

Another practice of the early brethren was the recitation of the

Office of the Virgin Mary. This devotional observance drew elements from the canonical Liturgy of the Hours, which the friars chanted daily in common in the chapel. Saint Dominic adopted the custom of praying the Office of the Virgin Mary, which was then said by the Cistercians and Premonstratensians.

But what did this observance mean for the early friars? One Dominican historian attests: Saint Dominic "arranged this in a special way. … So as not to make the liturgy burdensome, but to prepare for it and place it under the protection of the Mother of God, he had the brethren say the Hours of the Virgin Mary before the canonical Office."[9] Dominic intended for this set of prayers to Our Lady to be recited in the dormitory when the brethren arose, and then in the chapel before the other hours. In this way, the Virgin Mary was present throughout the daily lives and during prayers of the brethren.

THE HOLY ROSARY

For centuries the Church has attributed the origin and spread of the Rosary to Saint Dominic and his Order of Preachers. John Paul II writes, "The history of the Rosary shows how this prayer was used in particular by the Dominicans at a difficult time for the Church due to the spread of heresy."[10]

According to this tradition, Our Lady appeared to Dominic, who was desperate for heavenly aid in his preaching against the Albigensians, and instructed him to preach the mysteries of her life and holiness.

The practice of reciting the angel's greeting to Mary at the Annunciation (see Lk 1:28) dates to the eleventh century. For Saint Dominic and the early brethren, this would have been a familiar custom. The words of Elizabeth at the Visitation (Lk 1:42) were added sometime in the thirteenth century. These biblical phrases form the basis of the prayer we know as the Hail Mary.

At the same time, Christians were adopting and popularizing the custom of reciting 150 Our Fathers. The number 150 is significant, as it corresponds to the 150 psalms of the Bible. The recitation of the psalms forms the backbone of monastic and religious life, and the laity were encouraged to join themselves to that prayer by means of the repetition of Our Fathers. The prayers were counted on cords, called Paternosters, and divided into sets of 50. Hail Marys were added to the Our Fathers, as was the case when the Dominican General Chapter of 1266 legislated that lay brothers should pray both the Hail Mary and the Our Father in place of chanting the choral office.[11]

In the thirteenth century, then, there grew up the practice of reciting 150 Ave Marias. Connecting this devotion to Our Lady and the liturgical prayer of the Church, it became known by some as the Psalter of Mary. Blessed Romée of Livia, a companion of Saint Dominic and prior and provincial of the Dominican Order, died clutching his knotted cord, upon which he recited his Aves by the thousands. Dominicans wear a rosary at the waist, keeping Our Lady's prayer always at hand.

The Rosary is fundamentally a contemplative prayer. As we have said, Saint Dominic was known to speak always "to God or about God." Like the Virgin Mary herself, Dominic pondered the mysteries of the life of Christ in his heart (see Lk 2:19). Turning over and over again the great truths of the Faith, Dominic marveled at the love and mercy they continually reveal.

Further, the Rosary proclaims the reality of the Incarnation. With each Hail Mary, we profess the goodness of creation (of all that God has made), that Christ truly took human flesh, that family life is noble and virtuous. These and other professions of faith directly oppose the heresies of the Albigensians and those of their ilk. Thinking of Saint Dominic and his mission of preaching, Pope John Paul II notes, "Today we are facing new challenges. Why should we not once more have recourse to the

Rosary, with the same faith as those who have gone before us? The Rosary retains all its power and continues to be a valuable pastoral resource for every good evangelizer."[12]

A Gospel prayer, centered on the Incarnation and the redemption of Christ, the Rosary announces those saving truths that Dominic expounded so eloquently in his day.

Finally, the prayer of the Rosary conforms the one who prays to the life of Christ. Not only are the truths presented to be known, but the repetition and recitation fashions the heart of the one who prays after the heart of Christ. In this work of refashioning hearts, the Virgin Mary plays a pivotal role. Saint Louis de Montfort (a Third Order Dominican) writes:

> As all perfection consists in our being conformed, united and consecrated to Jesus it naturally follows that the most perfect of all devotions is that which conforms, unites, and consecrates us most completely to Jesus. Now of all God's creatures Mary is the most conformed to Jesus. It therefore follows that, of all devotions, devotion to her makes for the most effective consecration and conformity to him.[13]

The Rosary, which allows us to see the events of the life of Christ as Mary saw them, provides a pattern and form to unite our lives to Christ. In the spirit of their founder, the Dominicans' adoption and promotion of the Holy Rosary of the Blessed Virgin Mary is a profession of the central and unique role of Our Lady in salvation history. It is an expression of the Order's confidence in her continued care and bestowal of grace. And yet no less was the adoption of the Rosary a profound expression of the real and efficacious nature of prayer in which Saint Dominic himself so ardently believed.

MOTHER OF MERCY

One of the oldest prayers to the Virgin Mary is the ancient antiphon titled in Latin *Sub Tuum Praesidium*. By some accounts this prayer dates to the third century. The beautiful words, first written in Greek, present the Blessed Mother as one who intercedes for us. We turn to her, asking for her prayers, and she shows forth the graces of her Son:

> We fly to Thy protection,
> O Holy Mother of God;
> Do not despise our petitions
> in our necessities,
> but deliver us always
> from all dangers,
> O Glorious and Blessed Virgin.

The Order of Preachers adopted this powerful motif, Cistercian in origin, expressing a love for the Virgin of Mercy, who gathers her children under her mantle. The Virgin Mary is for us a mercy, a shield, a shelter.

According to Sister Cecilia of the monastery of Saint Sixtus (a cloistered nun who knew Saint Dominic), one night while Dominic was at prayer, he had a vision of heaven. As he gazed at rank upon rank of the heavenly host before the Lord, he did not see a single member of his own Order of Preachers. Distraught, he turned to Our Lord, who beckoned him to approach the Virgin Mary. "At this the Blessed Virgin drew back her mantle, and opening it wide before St Dominic, it seemed to enclose nearly the whole of that heavenly country, so vast was it, and beneath it he saw a great host of his brethren. Casting himself down, St Dominic returned hearty thanks to Christ and his holy mother."[14] As the story goes, when the vision faded, Dominic rang the bell for matins, prayed with the brethren, and then, calling them to the chapter room, he preached a sermon exhorting them to love and revere the Virgin Mary.

In imitation of Saint Dominic, not simply every Dominican but every follower of Christ should turn with confidence to the Blessed Mother. From her will pour forth a flood of heavenly grace, enough to quench the thirsty souls of this world. Guided by her intercession, we can continue courageously along the pilgrimage of this life, hoping to find ourselves, one day, rejoicing among the saints at her feet.

Conclusion
The Height of Heaven

A t six o'clock in the evening on August 6, 1221, Dominic de Guzman, just fifty-one years old, died in Bologna after a short illness. His death, like his life, bore witness to his incredible devotion to the Gospel of Christ. " 'He died in Brother Moneta's bed because he had none of his own; he died in Brother Moneta's tunic, because he had not another with which to replace the one he had long been wearing.' ... It sums up the detachment and poverty of his life. It pictures graphically the wandering mission of the greatest of Friars Preachers."[1]

When Saint Dominic died, his Order was not yet five years old. There was no way of knowing what would become of this new religious order of preaching friars. But Dominic did know that death was not an abandonment of everything he had established on earth. Fr. Bede Jarrett recounts the final moments of his life:

The lasting of his life was now only a question of hours. Rudolfo never left him, wiping from the still joyous face the sweat of death. As he began to enter into his agony, Dominic could not but notice the tearful eyes of those who stood about him; and the old courage and laughter prompted an answer that still consoles his sons: "Do not weep, beloved ones; do not sorrow that this frail body goes. I am going where I can serve you better."[2]

For centuries Saint Dominic has interceded for his Order from the heights of heaven. And from his intercession countless Dominicans have given their lives in service to Christ, in contemplation and study, in fraternity and observance, in dedication to the truth, and to the preaching of the Gospel. Such a life has produced some of the greatest saints the Church has ever known, and so many more whose names are known to God alone.

On his deathbed he continued to exhort his brothers: "Be eager in your service to God; strengthen and widen this new-born Order; increase your love of God and your keen observance of the rule; grow in holiness."[3] It is from these simple words that we can take our cue. The legacy of Saint Dominic is not realized in his ability to establish a religious order, or to study, or to preach well, though these are all part of him. Rather, it was his ability to bring souls to Christ.

For us, living eight hundred years after his death, this legacy is no less needed, no less vibrant, and no less accessible. What Saint Dominic offers to every Christian is not a path back to some nostalgic era of the Church but the means and the strength to build up the Church in our everyday lives, by clinging to the scriptures and feeding our minds with truth. He shows us that the Church is not rebuilt or reformed by turning away, but by men and women ready to die for her, by saints whose entire existence is wrapped up in the Church and is for the Church.

Dominic models a life full of prayer and contemplation, of deep and intimate friendship with Christ, which necessarily overflows into friendship and communion with others. He is also a witness of the freedom that is born of true, human love, not weighed down by the brokenness of this life. And, perhaps most importantly, his life teaches us that the goodness of the Father cannot be contained. It is contagious, good, and beautiful, and it must be shared.

The challenge for us, then, as it is for Christians of every age, is to cling continually to Christ, to be converted and healed by his grace. Saint Dominic's final words offer to us the way:

- "Be eager in your service to God." We are called to lay down our lives, as Christ did for us. "By this we know love, that he laid down his life for us; and we ought to lay down our lives for the brethren" (1 Jn 3:16). The paradox of our faith is that from self-offering, from death, comes life. There is no other way. The cross of Christ is the doorway to heaven. In virtue of our baptism and strengthened by our confirmation, we are called to imitate Christ in the offering of our lives so that, through his merits and grace, we may be conformed to him and may bear fruit for the Kingdom.
- "Strengthen and widen this new-born Order." Certainly, the Order of Preachers is no longer "newborn," but for so many in the world, the message of the Gospel is foreign. It is indeed the mission of the Order to preach the Gospel to all people. This missionary zeal comes from the heart of Saint Dominic, who desired to preach in non-Christian lands. Of course, some are called to missionary work. Some are not. All of us, though, can bear witness to the

truth of Christ in our families, places of work, and communities.

- "Increase your love of God." It is for this love that we are made — to know it, to live in it, and to love in return. To grow in love of God is simply the pursuit of the Christian life. It is the whole purpose of the Church, of the sacraments, of devotion, of our spiritual life, and of our service. After all, charity, as Saint Paul explains, is the greatest of virtues (see 1 Cor 13:13). Sometimes we think that religion is something for the weak and that speaking of a loving God is either incoherent in our current circumstances or just something to comfort those who cannot face life. Saint Dominic shows us by his way of life that he begs to differ. He knew that it was love that created, love that climbed the cross, love that rose from the dead, and love that re-creates in grace. This is what Saint Dominic preached.

- "Your keen observance of the rule." Consecrated religious profess vows to remain faithful to their way of life. Married men and women promise to remain faithful to one another until death. Each year at Easter, we renew our baptismal promises, reaffirming our belief in Christ and our adherence to him. "You, therefore, must be perfect, as your heavenly Father is perfect," Christ instructs (see Mt 5:48). Perfection is not something we can earn but is a grace given to us by God. We cooperate with that grace by remaining faithful and by encouraging others to do the same. These observances are not about accomplishing tasks on a checklist but are about availing ourselves of the Christian life, of what is good and salutary for us all.

- "Grow in holiness." What more could be said? The dying wish of Saint Dominic was that his brothers grow in holiness, in friendship with Christ. These words were spoken in Bologna eight hundred years ago, and they have continued to echo through the centuries. Dominic is, for us, a glorious witness of a life of holiness, filled with joy and happiness, with great friendship, and an unfailing zeal for the Gospel.

Prophecy is proven true with the passage of time, and it seems that Blessed Jane's vision of a dog carrying a torch in its mouth, setting the world ablaze with the love of the Gospel, has come true. Saint Dominic's life testifies to such a reality. What is more, those who follow his way of life, whether in the Order of Preachers or by taking Dominic as a patron, as an intercessor, and as an example, also fulfill this prophecy.

The words spoken by Saint Dominic's companions at his deathbed have resounded through the centuries, reminding us of Dominic's legacy and assuring us of his continued prayers:

> O Wonderful hope, which you gave to those who wept for you at the hour of your death, promising after your departure to be helpful to your brethren.
> Fulfill, O Father, what you have said, and help us by your prayers.

Epilogue

After eight hundred years, is there anything about Saint Dominic that is as yet undiscovered, unexplored, and unwritten? Over the centuries, is there anything that remains unreflected and unsaid about the founder and first friar of the Order of Preachers? Absent any new discovery of an ancient manuscript, it seems that a new book on Dominic would simply amount to an expanded footnote on everything that has already been written over the years. But before reaching this page, you, dear reader, must have already delightfully discovered something *new,* or perhaps, understood something *old* in a *new way.*

Saint Dominic embraced a mission that is *timely,* because he saw a world in dire need of a new evangelization; yet the same mission is truly *timeless,* because every generation is in want of a new evangelization — that is, the preaching of the One who is ever ancient, yet ever new. The "ancient yet new" paradox calls to mind the philosopher Hans-Georg Gadamer's notion of the classical. A "classic" is at once timeless and timely. It is timeless not because it lies beyond the vicissitudes of history but because it becomes an event of meaning in every moment of history. It is timely precisely because it is "a timeless present that is contemporaneous with every other present."[1] At the beginning of this book, the authors asked: *What could a medieval Spaniard offer my life today?*

Quaerere Deum, to seek to know and love God, with Saint Dominic as reliable guide, is the purpose of this remarkable book by our brothers Patrick Mary Briscoe, OP, and Jacob Bertrand Janczyk, OP. Hopefully, as you reach the end of this book, a desire to continue your search for God and the things of God has been awakened in you, not because you have not found God yet but because there is always something *more* in knowing and loving God. A member of Dominic's religious family, Saint Catherine of Siena, expressed this so beautifully: "You are a mystery as deep as the sea; the more I search, the more I find, and the more I find, the more I search for you. But I can never be satisfied; what I receive will ever leave me desiring more."[2]

The yearlong celebration of the eighth centenary of the birth of Saint Dominic into eternal life (August 6, 2021) started on the Solemnity of Epiphany (January 6, 2021) and will conclude on the same solemnity (January 6, 2022). This means that the beginning and conclusion of our celebration is an act of thanksgiving to God for the grace of his Epiphany, his revelation as *lumen gentium* (light to all the nations), especially to "seekers," like the "wise men from the East" (Mt 2:1–12), who went on pilgrimage to adore Emmanuel. The charism of Dominic is preaching the Gospel to all the nations, with the light of Christ to illumine his path. For us members of the Dominican family, the jubilee is a time to thank God for giving us Dominic, the founder and first friar of the Order of Preachers, whom we lovingly call *lumen ecclesiae* (light of the Church).

God first created light, and it is marvelous how the movement of many creatures is influenced by light. Scientists call this movement *phototaxis* — that is, a movement with respect to a light source. Positive phototaxis is movement toward the light; conversely, negative phototaxis is movement away from the light. Saint Dominic is *lumen ecclesiae* because his entire life was oriented toward Christ, *lumen gentium*. As light, Dominic is like the moon rather than the sun. Jesus is the only true light of the world, and just like all of us who are baptized in Christ, Dominic merely reflects the light of Christ. Interestingly, Dominic's mother, Blessed Jane, saw in a dream that Dominic had a moon on his forehead, and his godmother saw a star on his forehead at his baptism.[3] To radiate the light of Christ is what the Fathers of the Church call *lunar ministry* — to reflect the light of Christ, as the moon reflects the light of the sun. And we know that the brightness of moonshine depends on the moon's position in relation to the sun.

The brightness of the light we bear depends largely on our relation with Christ. Dominic is a brilliant *lumen ecclesiae* because his entire life is oriented and exposed to Christ; there is nothing that blocks the light of Christ, and so Dominic reflects this light more fully and brilliantly. Thankfully, Dominic did not keep to himself the spark of divine inspiration; he founded an Order of Preachers, an order of men and women dedicated to the *study of truth*, the *preaching of grace*, and the *building of communities*, especially the Church.

Toward the end of his life, Saint Dominic expressed his desire to be buried under the feet of the brethren.[4] Often, we think of such a wish as a manifestation of his profound humility. Yet we realize that, at that time, deeply devoted people wanted their mortal remains to be buried in a church, to be as close as possible to the altar, where the relics of saints rest, because closeness to the saints (in this case, to be within the vicinity of relics) signifies proximity to sanctity and salvation. Thus, when Dominic wanted to be buried "at the feet" of the preaching brothers, he wanted to be proximate to what constitutes, for him, a *path to sanctity* — that is, the preaching of the Gospel. Preachers are not necessarily holy, but preaching the Gospel brings us, as well as others, to the path of salvation.

We know that the charism of religious orders is not strictly unique to them. A charism is part of the "multiform grace of God," which makes the Church effective as a sacrament of salvation. Thus, it is important to realize that an essential aspect of the mission of an order or congregation that has received a particular charismatic gift is to awaken in all the faithful such a charism, which they share as members of the Church. Thus, a congregation whose charism is to take care of the sick calls our attention to the importance of this specific corporal work of mercy of the Church, including the *charism of healing* entrusted to the Church. Another congregation whose charism is to educate the young calls our attention to the importance of this spiritual work of mercy and the charism of the Church *as teacher*.

In the same vein, the charism of preaching given to Saint Dominic propelled him to remind the Church that her universal mission is to preach the Gospel and that preaching is a mission not of a few chosen ones but of all members of the Church. It is a charism shared by all the members of the Dominican family, brothers (ordained and lay), nuns, apostolic sisters, priestly fraternity, and lay Dominicans — all the states of life in the Church. As one wise cooperator brother said: We are not an Order of *homilists*, but an order of *preachers*!

Gerard Francisco Timoner III, OP
Master of the Order of Preachers and Successor of Saint Dominic
Solemnity of Saint Joseph
Rome, March 19, 2021

Notes

PREFACE

1. Emily Boerger, "CDC Reports: One in Four Young Adults Contemplated Suicide during COVID-19 Pandemic," State of Reform, August 14, 2020, accessed March 1, 2021, https://stateofreform.com /news/2020/08/cdc-reports-one-in-four-young-adults-contemplated -suicide-during-covid-19-pandemic/.

2. "Quotes for Sunday Bulletins," Diocese of Springfield in Illinois, accessed March 17, 2021, https://www.dio.org/uploads/files /Communications/Parish_Link/Quotes_for_Sunday_Bulletins.pdf.

3. Francis, *Evangelii Gaudium*, pars. 89, 7, accessed March 17, 2021, Vatican.va.

4. Benedict XVI, *Spe Salvi*, par. 30, accessed March 17, 2021, Vatican.va.

5. Joseph Ratzinger, *Truth and Tolerance* (San Francisco: Ignatius Press, 2004), 137.

6. Colman E. O'Neill, OP, *Sacramental Realism* (Wilmington, DE:

Michael Glazier, 1983), 32.

7. Benedict XVI, General Audience (February 3, 2010), accessed March 17, 2021, Vatican.va.

8. Guy Bedouelle, *Saint Dominic: The Grace of the Word*, trans. Mary Thomas Noble (San Francisco: Ignatius Press, 1987), 20.

9. Jordan of Saxony, "The Libellus of Jordan of Saxony," in *St. Dominic: Biographical Documents*, ed. Francis Lehner (Washington, DC: Thomist Press, 1964), 34.

10. H. D. Lacordaire, *The Life of Saint Dominic*, trans. Edward Hazeland (London: Burns and Oates, 1883), 21–22.

11. Hans Urs von Balthasar, *Bernanos* (San Francisco: Ignatius Press, 1996), 315, 316.

12. Letter of John Paul II to the Master General of the Order of Preachers, June 28, 2001, accessed March 17, 2021, Vatican.va.

CHAPTER 1: Living in the Word

1. Jean de Mailly, "The Life of St. Dominic," in *Early Dominicans: Selected Writings*, ed. Simon Tugwell (Mahwah, NJ: Paulist Press, 1982), 53.

2. John Paul II, *Familiaris Consortio*, par. 39, accessed March 17, 2021, Vatican.va.

3. Jordan of Saxony, "The Libellus," 10.

4. Bedouelle, *Saint Dominic*, 65.

5. Paul Murray, *The New Wine of Dominican Spirituality: A Drink Called Happiness* (London: Burns and Oates, 2006), 83.

6. Simon Tugwell, "The Canonization Process of St. Dominic 1233," in *Early Dominicans*, 72.

7. Ibid., 75.

8. Ibid.

9. Ibid., 83.

10. *Book of Constitutions and Ordinations of the Brothers of the Order of Preachers* (Dublin: Dominican Publications, 2012) (hereafter cited as *LCO*), 28.I.

11. "Constitution of Nuns of the Order of Preachers," 98.I.

12. *John Cassian: The Conferences,* Ancient Christian Writers, no. 57, trans. Boniface Ramsey (New York: Newman Press, 1997), 14.XI.1, 515.

13. Second Vatican Council, *Dei Verbum,* par. 25, accessed March 17, 2021, Vatican.va (hereafter cited as *DV*).

14. Francis, *Aperuit Illis,* par. 12, accessed March 17, 2021, Vatican.va.

15. Second Vatican Council, *Sacrosanctum Concilium,* par. 7, accessed March 17, 2021, Vatican.va (hereafter cited as *SC*).

16. Ibid., par. 84.

17. Ibid., par. 85.

18. John Paul II, General Audience (April 4, 2001), accessed March 17, 2021, Vatican.va.

19. Simon Tugwell, *The Nine Ways of Prayer of Saint Dominic* (Dublin: Dominican Publications, 1978), 42.

20. Ibid., 26.

21. Ibid.

22. Cassian, *The Conferences,* 14.X.1, 513–14.

CHAPTER 2: Given to Truth

1. Catherine of Siena, *The Dialogue,* Classics of Western Spirituality, trans. Suzanne Noffke (New York: Paulist Press, 1980), 337.

2. Aristotle, *Metaphysics,* 1011b25.

3. Thomas Aquinas, *Summa Theologica,* trans. Fathers of the English Dominican Province (New York: Benzinger Brothers, 1911–1925), Ia, q.16, a.1.

4. Joseph Ratzinger, Homily (April 18, 2005), accessed March 17, 2021, Vatican.va.

5. Bedouelle, *Saint Dominic,* 168.

6. Bede Jarrett, *The Life of Saint Dominic* (Providence, RI: Cluny Media, 2018), 17.

7. Jordan of Saxony, "The Libellus," 13.

8. Murray, *The New Wine of Dominican Spirituality*, 85.

9. Jarrett, *The Life of Saint Dominic*, 82.

10. Jordan of Saxony, "The Libellus," 41.

11. Ralph Francis Bennett, *The Early Dominicans: Studies in Thirteenth-Century Dominican History*, Cambridge Studies in Medieval Life and Thought, ed. G. Coulton (Cambridge, UK: University Press, 1937), 24.

12. Bedouelle, *Saint Dominic*, 164.

13. Gerard de Frachet, *The Legend of St. Dominic*, 25.

14. "The Process of Canonization at Bologna," in *St. Dominic: Biographical Documents*, ed. Francis C. Lehner (Washington, DC: Thomist Press, 1964), 123.

15. Ibid., 118.

16. A. G. Sertillanges, *The Intellectual Life: Its Spirit, Conditions, Methods*, trans. Mary Ryan (Washington, DC: Catholic University of America Press, 1987), preface.

17. Ibid.

18. Ibid., 133.

19. Humbert of Romans, "Treatise on the Formation of Preachers," in *Early Dominicans: Selected Writings*, ed. Simon Tugwell (Mahwah, NJ: Paulist Press, 1982), 205.

20. Ibid., 190.

21. John Paul II, *Veritatis Splendor*, par. 1, accessed March 17, 2021, Vatican.va.

22. Benedict XVI, *Caritas in Veritate*, par. 1, accessed March 17, 2021, Vatican.va.

23. Aquinas, *Summa Theologica*, IIIa, q.42, a.4.

24. Jordan of Saxony, "The Libellus," 73.

CHAPTER 3: Within the Fold

1. Bedouelle, *Saint Dominic*, 193.

2. Second Vatican Council, "Dogmatic Constitution on the Church, *Lumen gentium*, 21 November, 1964," in *Vatican Council II: The Con-*

ciliar and Post Conciliar Documents, ed. Austin Flannery (Collegeville, MN: Liturgical Press, 1975), par. 3 (hereafter cited as *LG*).

3. Clement of Alexandria, *Paedagogus* 1, 6, 27: PG 8, 281. As quoted in the *Catechism of the Catholic Church*, 2nd ed. (Vatican City: Libreria Editrice Vaticana, 2000) (hereafter cited as CCC), 760.

4. James of Voragine and William Granger Ryan, *The Golden Legend: Readings on the Saints* (Princeton, NJ: Princeton University Press, 1995), 46.

5. Georges Bernanos, *Saint Dominic*, trans. Anthony Giambrone (Providence, RI: Cluny Media, 2017), 37.

6. William A. Hinnebusch, *The History of the Dominican Order: Origins and Growth to 1500* (Staten Island, NY: Alba House, 1966), 77.

7. "The Process of Canonization at Bologna," 144.

8. St. Augustine, *Commentary on the Gospel of John* 21:8.

9. "The Process of Canonization at Bologna," 127.

10. Benedict XVI, General Audience (April 13, 2011), accessed March 17, 2021, Vatican.va.

11. Thomas Aquinas, *Commentary on the Creed*, a.9.

12. Paul VI, *Solemni Hac Liturgia,* par. 19, accessed March 17, 2021, Vatican.va.

13. Jordan of Saxony, "The Libellus," 23.

14. Francis, General Audience (October 9, 2011), accessed March 17, 2021, Vatican.va.

15. William A. Hinnebusch, *Dominican Spirituality* (Eugene, OR: Wipf & Stock, 2014), 59.

16. *DV*, par. 7.

17. Paul VI, *Ecclesiam Suam,* par. 46, accessed March 17, 2021, Vatican.va.

18. *LG*, par. 25.

19. Bedouelle, *Saint Dominic*, 121.

20. Jarrett, *The Life of Saint Dominic*, 97.

21. Aquinas, *Commentary on the Creed*, a.9.

CHAPTER 4: Mystical Union

1. Aquinas, *Summa Theologica*, IIa-IIae, q.188, a.6.
2. Jordan of Saxony, "The Libellus," 77.
3. LCO, 56 (emphasis added).
4. Ibid., 66.
5. Réginald Garrigou-Lagrange, *Knowing the Love of God: Lessons from a Spiritual Master* (DeKalb, IL: Lighthouse Catholic Media, 2015), 158.
6. "The Process of Canonization at Bologna," 95–135.
7. *LG*, par. 40.
8. Jarrett, *The Life of St. Dominic*, 110.
9. Ibid., 114.

CHAPTER 5: Friendship unto Heaven

1. *LCO*, 2.I.
2. Ibid., 4.I.
3. Jordan of Saxony, "The Libellus," 76.
4. "The Process of Canonization at Bologna," 129.
5. Ibid., 120.
6. Aquinas, *Summa Theologica*, Ia-IIae, q.4, a.8.
7. Ibid.
8. Ibid., ad3.
9. CCC 2204, 2206.
10. Thomas Aquinas, *Summa Contra Gentiles: Books III–IV*, trans. Laurence Shapcote (Green Bay, WI: Aquinas Institute, 2018), III, 123, 6.

CHAPTER 6: Free to Love

1. "The Process of Canonization at Bologna," 131.
2. Ibid., 102.
3. Aquinas, *Summa Theologica*, Ia-IIae, q.56, a.4.
4. John Paul II, *Vita Consecrata*, par. 21, accessed March 17, 2021, Vatican.va.

CHAPTER 7: Mission to Witness

1. Honorius III, "The Bulls of Approbation," in *St. Dominic: Biographical Documents*, ed. Francis C. Lehner (Washington, DC: Thomist Press, 1964), 198.

2. Ibid., 201.

3. Ibid., 202.

4. Jordan of Saxony, "The Libellus," 7.

5. Ibid., 13.

6. Ibid., 43.

7. Humbert of Romans, *Treatise on Preaching*, ed. Walter Conlon (Westminster, MD: Newman Press, 1955), 31.

8. Humbert Clerissac, *The Spirit of St. Dominic* (Providence, RI: Cluny Media, 2015), 12.

9. Second Vatican Council, *Gaudium et Spes*, par. 22, accessed March 17, 2021, Vatican.va.

10. Peter John Cameron, *Why Preach: Encountering Christ in God's World* (San Francisco: Ignatius Press, 2009), 130.

11. Jordan of Saxony, *On the Beginnings of the Order of Preachers*, trans. Simon Tugwell (Chicago: Parable, 1982), 16.

CHAPTER 8: Under the Virgin's Mantle

1. Pius V, *Consueverunt Romani* (1569), par. 1.

2. Gérard de Frachet, *Lives of the Brethren of the Order of Preachers, 1206–1259: The Dominicans*, ed. Bede Jarrett (London: Blackfriars Publications, 1955), 5.

3. Thomas of Cantimpré, "Defense of the Mendicants," in *Early Dominicans: Selected Writings*, ed. Simon Tugwell (Mahwah, NJ: Paulist Press, 1982), 136.

4. Marie-Humbert Vicaire, *Saint Dominic and His Times*, trans. Kathleen Pond (New York: McGraw-Hill, 1964), 116.

5. Jordan of Saxony, "The Libellus," 50.

6. Bedouelle, *Saint Dominic*, 251.

7. Jordan of Saxony, "The Libellus," 82.

8. Frachet, *Lives of the Brethren*, 108.

9. Bedouelle, *Saint Dominic*, 252.

10. John Paul II, *Rosarium Virginis Mariae*, par. 17, accessed March 17, 2021, Vatican.va.

11. Bedouelle, *Saint Dominic*, 254.

12. John Paul II, *Rosarium Virginis Mariae*, par. 17.

13. St. Louis de Montfort, *True Devotion to Mary*, trans. Fr. Frederick Faber (Rockford, IL: TAN Books, 1985), 77.

14. Frachet, *Lives of the Brethren*, 82.

CONCLUSION

1. Jarrett, *The Life of St. Dominic*, 172.

2. Ibid., 170–71.

3. Ibid., 169.

EPILOGUE

1. Hans-Georg Gadamer, *Truth and Method*, trans. Joel Weinnsheimer and Donald G. Marshall (New York: Crossroad, 1989), 288.

2. Catherine of Siena, *The Dialogue*, 364.

3. Jordan of Saxony, "The Libellus," 9.

4. "The Process of Canonization at Bologna," 8.

About the Authors

A native of Fort Wayne, Indiana, Fr. Patrick Mary Briscoe, OP, joined the Order of Preachers in 2010. Following his ordination to the priesthood, he was assigned in Providence, Rhode Island. Father Patrick has served as a college chaplain and instructor of theology at Providence College and as a parish priest at St. Pius V Church. Interested in new media and the work of the new evangelization, he is a host of the podcast *Godsplaining* and an editor of the Catholic news website Aleteia.org.

Fr. Jacob Bertrand Janczyk, OP, is the director of vocations for the Dominican Province of St. Joseph. He entered the Order of Preachers in 2010 and was ordained to the priesthood in 2017. Following his ordination, Father Jacob Bertrand served as the assistant chaplain at Aquinas House, the Catholic campus ministry at Dartmouth College. He is also a host of the podcast *Godsplaining*.